IN THE SAME SERIES

UNDERSTANDING NEWS
John Hartley

ADVERTISING AS COMMUNICATION
Gillian Dyer

CASE STUDIES AND PROJECTS IN COMMUNICATION
Neil McKeown

KEY CONCEPTS IN COMMUNICATION
*Tim O'Sullivan,
John Hartley, Danny Saunders and John Fiske*

AN INTRODUCTION TO LANGUAGE AND SOCIETY
Martin Montgomery

POPULAR CULTURE:
THE METROPOLITAN EXPERIENCE
Iain Chambers

UNDERSTANDING RADIO
Andrew Crisell

TELEVISION DRAMA:
AGENCY, AUDIENCE AND MYTH
John Tulloch

UNDERSTANDING TELEVISION
Andrew Goodwin and Garry Whannel

FILM AS SOCIAL PRACTICE
Graeme Turner

ON VIDEO
Roy Armes

INTRODUCTION TO COMMUNICATION STUDIES

Second edition

John Fiske

ROUTLEDGE

London and New York

P
90
.F58
1990

First published in 1982 by
Methuen & Co. Ltd
Reprinted nine times
Second edition published 1990
by Routledge
11 New Fetter Lane, London EC4P 4EE

Simultaneously published in the USA and Canada
by Routledge
a division of Routledge, Chapman and Hall, Inc.
29 West 35th Street, New York, NY 10001

Typeset in 10/12pt Baskerville by Columns of Reading

Printed in Great Britain by Guernsey Press Co Ltd

British Library Cataloguing in Publication Data
Fiske, John
    Introduction to communication studies. — 2nd ed —
    (Studies in culture and communication)
    1. Man. Communication
    I. Title   II. Series
    001.51

Library of Congress Cataloging in Publication Data
Fiske, John
    Introduction to communication studies / John Fiske. — New ed.
        p.   cm. — (Studies in culture and communication)
    Includes bibliographical references.
    1. Communication.   2. Semiotics.   I. Title.   II. Series.
P90.F58   1990
302.2—dc20   89–24187

ISBN 0 415 04671 8 hbk 2nd edition
ISBN 0 415 04672 6 pbk 2nd edition

(ISBN 0 416 74560 1 hbk 1st edition)
(ISBN 0 415 02780 2 pbk 1st edition)

To NATASHA
for everything

To MATTHEW AND LUCY
for keeping quiet (well . . . fairly)
during the cold wet summer of 1980

CONTENTS

84692

CONTENTS

LIST OF PLATES

ACKNOWLEDGEMENTS

Many people have contributed directly or indirectly to this book. But my thanks must go first to my students on the BA Communication Studies course at the Polytechnic of Wales: you have deflated, deflected, and sharpened my ideas, you have produced ideas of your own, and you have teased me out of (most of) my jargon.

To my colleagues on the staff I am indebted for specific comments, but, more importantly, for providing the sort of environment that encourages ideas to develop.

Ray Bailey and Brian Dibble of the Western Australian Institute of Technology, Perth, and Richard Dimbleby and his group of communication lecturers in FE have all given valuable feedback.

To Viv Coles for photography and to Jenny Griffiths for typing: your concrete identifiable contributions were essential.

And finally to my family, who allowed too many weekends and vacations to be organized around this book: thank you.

The publishers and I would also like to thank the following for their permission to reproduce the illustrations in the text: Syndication International for plates 1a and b; the Board of Trustees of the University of Illinois Press for figure 2; *The Guardian*, John Kent, and Paul Raymond Publications Ltd for plate 4; *Punch* for plate 6; B. Westley, M. Maclean, and *Journalism Quarterly* for figures 7, 8, and 9; Hutchinsons for plate 7; Gallaher Ltd for plate 8; Cockman Thompson Wilding and Co. for plate 9; Pasta Foods Ltd for plate 10; *The Observer* for plates 11a and b; *The Sunday Times* for plate 12; the BBC for plates 14, 15a, and 15b; the English Tourist Board for plate 17; Eve Arnold for plate 18; and G. Gerbner and The Annals of the American Association of Political and

Social Science for figure 26. Every effort has been made to contact copyright holders; where this has not been possible we apologize to those concerned.

J. F.

GENERAL EDITOR'S PREFACE

This series of books on different aspects of communication is designed to meet the needs of the growing number of students coming to study this subject for the first time. The authors are experienced teachers or lecturers who are committed to bridging the gap between the huge body of research available to more advanced students, and what new students actually need to get them started on their studies.

Probably the most characteristic feature of communication is its diversity: it ranges from the mass media and popular culture, through language to individual and social behaviour. But it identifies links and a coherence within this diversity. The series will reflect the structure of its subject. Some books will be general, basic works that seek to establish theories and methods of study applicable to a wide range of material; others will apply these theories and methods to the study of one particular topic. But even these topic-centred books will relate to each other, as well as to the more general ones. One particular topic, such as advertising or news or language, can only be understood as an example of communication when it is related to, and differentiated from, all the other topics that go to make up this diverse subject.

The series, then, has two main aims, both closely connected. The first is to introduce readers to the most important results of contemporary research into communication together with the theories that seek to explain it. The second is to equip them with appropriate methods of study and investigation which they will be able to apply directly to their everyday experience of communication.

If readers can write better essays, produce better projects, and pass more exams as a result of reading these books I shall be very satisfied; but if they gain a new insight into how communication shapes and informs our social life, how it articulates and creates our experience of industrial society, then I shall be delighted. Communication is too often taken for granted when it should be taken to pieces.

John Fiske

AUTHOR'S NOTE

Strategies for reading this book

Chapters 1 to 5 are devoted to introducing the reader to the main models, theories, and concepts used in the study of communication. I have, where it seemed appropriate, covered this material in sections headed *Basic concept(s)* and *Further implications*. The reader wanting a brief, general introduction to the subject can read the 'basic concept' sections only. If s/he wishes to dig further, the 'further implications' sections are there for the reading. Teachers who feel that 'the process school' offers the easier way into the subject may wish to turn first to chapters 1, 2, the early part of 4, and 8, before returning to cover the more theoretical and conceptual work of the semiotic school. But I hope most readers will read the book in the order in which it was written: this should give their introductory studies both balance and depth.

Suggestions for further work and reading

At the end of each chapter I have suggested topics for discussion or essay writing, or practical exercises. These are designed to test, follow up, or deepen the reader's understanding of the chapter. They are not comprehensive, and I am sure many readers will devise better ones for themselves.

I have also suggested further reading. This is not essential, for all the further work suggested can be adequately undertaken on a reading of this book alone. But other books are always helpful. I have tried to refer to the literature selectively, not comprehensively. I have also tried to restrict my references to books in print and in paperback. The ones referred to most frequently in the suggestions for further work are listed at the start of the bibliography. I will certainly have omitted books that are at least as useful as the ones I have selected: the omission does not imply a value judgement.

INTRODUCTION
WHAT IS
COMMUNICATION?

Communication is one of those human activities that everyone recognizes but few can define satisfactorily. Communication is talking to one another, it is television, it is spreading information, it is our hair style, it is literary criticism: the list is endless. This is one of the problems facing academics: can we properly apply the term 'a subject of study' to something as diverse and multi-faceted as human communication actually is? Is there any hope of linking the study of, say, facial expression with literary criticism? Is it even an exercise worth attempting?

The doubts that lie behind questions like these may give rise to the view that communication is not a subject, in the normal academic sense of the word, but is a multi-disciplinary area of study. This view would propose that what the psychologists and sociologists have to tell us about human communicative behaviour has very little to do with what the literary critic has.

This lack of agreement about the nature of communication studies is necessarily reflected in this book. What I have tried to do is to give some coherence to the confusion by basing the book upon the following assumptions.

I assume that communication is amenable to study, but that we need a number of disciplinary approaches to be able to study it comprehensively.

I assume that all communication involves signs and codes. Signs are artefacts or acts that refer to something other than themselves; that is, they are signifying constructs. Codes are the systems into which signs are organized and which determine how signs may be related to each other.

1

I assume, too, that these signs and codes are transmitted or made available to others: and that transmitting or receiving signs/codes/communication is the practice of social relationships.

I assume that communication is central to the life of our culture: without it culture of any kind must die. Consequently the study of communication involves the study of the culture with which it is integrated.

Underlying these assumptions is a general definition of communication as 'social interaction through messages'.

The structure of this book reflects the fact that there are two main schools in the study of communication. The first sees communication as the *transmission of messages*. It is concerned with how senders and receivers encode and decode, with how transmitters use the channels and media of communication. It is concerned with matters like efficiency and accuracy. It sees communication as a process by which one person affects the behaviour or state of mind of another. If the effect is different from or smaller than that which was intended, this school tends to talk in terms of communication failure, and to look to the stages in the process to find out where the failure occurred. For the sake of convenience I shall refer to this as the 'process' school.

The second school sees communication as the *production and exchange of meanings*. It is concerned with how messages, or texts, interact with people in order to produce meanings; that is, it is concerned with the role of texts in our culture. It uses terms like signification, and does not consider misunderstandings to be necessarily evidence of communication failure – they may result from cultural differences between sender and receiver. For this school, the study of communication is the study of text and culture. The main method of study is semiotics (the science of signs and meanings), and that is the label I shall use to identify this approach.

The process school tends to draw upon the social sciences, psychology and sociology in particular, and tends to address itself to *acts* of communication. The semiotic school tends to draw upon linguistics and the arts subjects, and tends to address itself to *works* of communication.

Each school interprets our definition of communication as social interaction through messages in its own way. The first defines social interaction as the process by which one person relates to others, or affects the behaviour, state of mind or emotional response of another, and, of course, vice versa. This is close to the common-sense, everyday use of the phrase. Semiotics, however, defines social interaction as that which constitutes the individual as a member of a particular culture or society. I know I am a member of western, industrial society because, to give one of many sources of identification, I respond to Shakespeare or *Coronation Street* in broadly the same ways as do the fellow members of my culture. I also become aware of cultural differences if, for instance, I hear a Soviet critic reading *King Lear* as a devastating attack upon the western ideal of the family as the basis of society, or arguing that *Coronation Street* shows how the west keeps the workers in their place. Both these readings are possible, but my point is, they are not mine, as a typical member of my culture. In responding to *Coronation Street* in the more normal way, I am expressing my commonality with other members of my culture. So, too, teenagers appreciating one particular style of rock music are expressing their identity as members of a subculture and are, albeit in an indirect way, interacting with other members of their society.

The two schools also differ in their understanding of what constitutes a message. The process school sees a message as that which is transmitted by the communication process. Many of its followers believe that intention is a crucial factor in deciding what constitutes a message. Thus pulling my earlobe would not be a message unless I deliberately did it as a pre-arranged signal to an auctioneer. The sender's intention may be stated or unstated, conscious or unconscious, but must be retrievable by analysis. The message is what the sender puts into it by whatever means.

For semiotics, on the other hand, the message is a construction of signs which, through interacting with the receivers, produce meanings. The sender, defined as transmitter of the message, declines in importance. The emphasis shifts to the text and how it is 'read'. And reading is the process of discovering meanings that occurs when the reader interacts or negotiates with the text. This negotiation takes place as the reader brings aspects of his or her cultural experience to bear upon the codes and signs which make up the text. It also involves some shared understanding of what the text is about. We have only to see how different papers report the same event differently to realize how important is this understanding, this view of the world, which each paper shares with its readers. So readers with different social experiences or from different cultures may find different meanings in the same text. This is not, as we have said, necessarily evidence of communication failure.

The message, then, is not something sent from A to B, but an element in a structured relationship whose other elements include external reality and the producer/reader. Producing and reading the text are seen as parallel, if not identical, processes in that they occupy the same place in this structured relationship. We might model this structure as a triangle

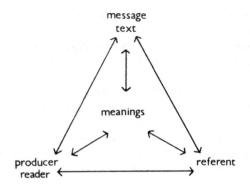

Figure 1   *Messages and meanings*

in which the arrows represent constant interaction; the structure is not static but a dynamic practice (see figure 1).

In this book I have tried to introduce the student to the work of the main authorities in each school. I have also tried to show how one school may illuminate or compensate for gaps or weaknesses in the other; or conversely where the two schools may be at loggerheads, where they may contradict or even undermine each other. Certainly I wish to encourage students to adopt a critical stance in their studies; that is, to be critically aware of their *method* of study as well as their *subject* of study, and to be able to articulate why they are studying communication in the way that they are.

I believe, then, that the student needs to draw upon both schools in order to approach the heart of the matter. The reader who wishes to identify the work of each as it is covered in this book may find the following account of the book's structure useful.

The structure of this book

Chapters 1 and 2 study a representative range of the models of communication produced by the process school. Then chapter 3 moves on to consider the roles of signs and meaning: this contains the theoretical base of semiotics. Then in chapter 4 we turn our attention to the codes into which signs are organized. Both schools are concerned with codes: the process school sees them as the means of encoding and decoding, whereas semiotics sees them as systems of meaning. The study of semiotic theory is further developed in chapter 5 when we study the ways in which signs signify within a culture. Chapters 6 and 8 are devoted to practical applications: chapter 6 to demonstrations of semiotic analysis, and chapter 8 to examples of empirical studies of message content and of the audience. These were carried out by members of the process school. Chapter 7 introduces some basic ideas of structuralism and shows how they may be applied. Chapter 9 addresses itself to the final and most abstract concern of semiotics — the role of ideology in meaning.

But within this structure I have taken every opportunity to compare the two schools; and I make no apologies for the fact that comments from the process school will appear in semiotic chapters and vice versa, for this is the best way of bringing the two schools into perspective.

1 COMMUNICATION THEORY

Origins

Shannon and Weaver's *Mathematical Theory of Communication* (1949; Weaver, 1949b) is widely accepted as one of the main seeds out of which Communication Studies has grown. It is a clear example of the process school, seeing communication as the transmission of messages.

Their work developed during the Second World War in the Bell Telephone Laboratories in the US, and their main concern was to work out a way in which the *channels* of communication could be used most efficiently. For them, the main channels were the telephone cable and the radio wave. They produced a theory that enabled them to approach the problem of how to send a maximum amount of information along a given channel, and how to measure the capacity of any one channel to carry information. This concentration on the channel and its capacity is appropriate to their engineering and mathematical background, but they claim that their theory is widely applicable over the whole question of human communication.

Shannon and Weaver's model (1949; Weaver, 1949b)

Their basic model of communication presents it as a simple linear process. Its simplicity has attracted many derivatives, and its linear, process-centred nature has attracted many critics. But we must look at the model (figure 2) before we consider its implications and before we attempt to evaluate it. The model is broadly understandable at first glance. Its obvious characteristics of simplicity and linearity stand out clearly. We will return to the named elements in the process later.

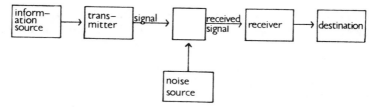

Figure 2   *Shannon and Weaver's model of communication*

Shannon and Weaver identify three levels of problems in the study of communication. These are:

Level A   How accurately can the symbols of
(technical problems) communication be transmitted?

Level B   How precisely do the transmitted symbols
(semantic problems)   convey the desired meaning?

Level C   How effectively does the received meaning
(effectiveness problems) affect conduct in the desired way?

The technical problems of level A are the simplest to understand and these are the ones that the model was originally developed to explain.

The semantic problems are again easy to identify, but much harder to solve, and range from the meaning of words to the meaning that a US newsreel picture might have for a Russian. Shannon and Weaver consider that the meaning is contained in the message: thus improving the encoding will increase the semantic accuracy. But there are also cultural factors at work here which the model does not specify: the meaning is at least as much in the culture as in the message.

The effectiveness problems may at first sight seem to imply that Shannon and Weaver see communication as manipulation or propaganda: that A has communicated effectively with B when B responds in the way A desires. They do lay themselves open to this criticism, and hardly deflect it by claiming that the aesthetic or emotional response to a work of art is an *effect* of communication.

They claim that the three levels are not watertight, but are interrelated, and interdependent, and that their model, despite its origin in level A, works equally well on all three levels. The point of studying communication at each and all of these levels is to understand how we may improve the *accuracy* and *efficiency* of the process.

But let us return to our model. The *source* is seen as the decision maker; that is, the source decides which message to send, or rather selects one out of a set of possible messages. This selected message is then changed

7

by the *transmitter* into a *signal* which is sent through the *channel* to the *receiver*. For a telephone the channel is a wire, the signal an electrical current in it, and the transmitter and receiver are the telephone handsets. In conversation, my mouth is the transmitter, the signal is the sound waves which pass through the channel of the air (I could not talk to you in a vacuum), and your ear is the receiver.

Obviously, some parts of the model can operate more than once. In the telephone message for instance, my mouth transmits a signal to the handset which is at this moment a receiver, and which instantly becomes a transmitter to send the signal to your handset, which receives it and then transmits it via the air to your ear. Gerbner's model, as we will see later, deals more satisfactorily with this doubling up of certain stages of the process.

Noise

The one term in the model whose meaning is not readily apparent is noise. Noise is anything that is added to the signal between its transmission and reception that is not intended by the source. This can be distortion of sound or crackling in a telephone wire, static in a radio signal, or 'snow' on a television screen. These are all examples of noise occurring within the channel and this sort of noise, on level A, is Shannon and Weaver's main concern. But the concept of noise has been extended to mean any signal received that was not transmitted by the source, or anything that makes the intended signal harder to decode accurately. Thus an uncomfortable chair during a lecture can be a source of noise — we do not receive messages through our eyes and ears only. Thoughts that are more interesting than the lecturer's words are also noise.

Shannon and Weaver admit that the level-A concept of noise needs extending to cope with level-B problems. They distinguish between semantic noise (level B) and engineering noise (level A) and suggest that a box labelled 'semantic receiver' may need inserting between the engineering receiver and the destination. Semantic noise is defined as any distortion of meaning occurring in the communication process which is not intended by the source but which affects the reception of the message at its destination.

Noise, whether it originates in the channel, the audience, the sender, or the message itself, always confuses the intention of the sender and thus limits the amount of desired information that can be sent in a given situation in a given time. Overcoming the problems caused by noise led Shannon and Weaver into some further fundamental concepts.

Information: basic concept

Despite their claims to operate on levels A, B, and C, Shannon and Weaver do, in fact, concentrate their work on level A. On this level, their term information is used in a specialist, technical sense, and to understand it we must erase from our minds its usual everyday meaning.

Information on level A is a measure of the predictability of the signal, that is the number of choices open to its sender. It has nothing to do with its content. A signal, we remember, is the physical form of a message – sound waves in the air, light waves, electrical impulses, touchings, or whatever. So, I may have a code that consists of two signals – a single flash of a light bulb, or a double flash. The *information* contained by either of these signals is identical – 50 per cent predictability. This is regardless of what they actually mean – one flash could mean 'Yes', two flashes 'No', or one flash could mean the whole of the Old Testament, and two flashes the New. In this case 'Yes' contains the same amount of information as the 'Old Testament'. The information contained by the letter 'u' when it follows the letter 'q' in English is nil because it is totally predictable.

Information: further implications

We can use the unit 'bit' to measure information. The word 'bit' is a compression of 'binary digit' and means, in practice, a Yes/No choice. These binary choices, or binary oppositions, are the basis of computer language, and many psychologists claim that they are the way in which our brain operates too. For instance, if we wish to assess someone's age we go through a rapid series of binary choices: are they old or are they young; if young, are they adult or pre-adult; if pre-adult, are they teenager or pre-teenager; if pre-teenager, are they school-age or pre-school; if pre-school, are they toddler or baby? The answer is baby. Here, in this system of binary choices the word 'baby' contains five bits of information because we have made five choices along the way. Here, of course, we have slipped easily on to level B, because these are semantic categories, or categories of meaning, not simply of signal. 'Information' at this level is much closer to our normal use of the term. So if we say someone is young we give one bit of information only, that he is not old. If we say he is a baby we give five bits of information *if*, and it is a big *if*, we use the classifying system detailed above.

This is the trouble with the concept of 'information' on level B. The semantic systems are not so precisely defined as are the signal systems of level A, and thus the numerical measuring of information is harder, and some would say irrelevant. There is no doubt that a letter (i.e. part of the signal system of level A) contains five bits of information. (Ask if it is in the first or second half of the alphabet, then in the first or second half of the half you have chosen, and so on. Five questions, or binary choices, will enable you to identify any letter in the alphabet.) But there is considerable doubt about the possibility of measuring meaning in the same sort of way.

Obviously, Shannon and Weaver's engineering and mathematical background shows in their emphasis. In the design of a telephone system, the critical factor is the number of signals it can carry. *What* people actually say is irrelevant. The question for us, however, is how useful a theory with this sort of mechanistic base can be in the broader study of communication. Despite the doubts about the value of measuring meaning and information numerically, relating the amount of information to the number of choices available is insightful, and is broadly similar to insights into the nature of language provided by linguistics and semiotics, as we will see later in this book. Notions of predictability and choice are vital in understanding communication.

Redundancy and entropy

Redundancy: basic concepts

Closely related to 'information' is the concept of *redundancy*. Redundancy is that which is predictable or conventional in a message. The opposite of redundancy is *entropy*. Redundancy is the result of high predictability, entropy of low predictability. So a message with low predictability can be said to be entropic and of high information. Conversely, a message of high predictability is redundant and of low information. If I meet a friend in the street and say 'Hello', I have a highly predictable, highly redundant message.

But I have not wasted my time and effort. The layman's use of the term to imply uselessness is misleading. Redundancy is not merely useful in communication, it is absolutely vital. In theory, communication *can* take place without redundancy, but in practice the situations in which this is possible are so rare as to be non-existent. A degree of redundancy is essential to practical communication. The English language is about 50 per cent redundant. This means we can delete about 50 per cent of the words and still have a usable language capable of transmitting understandable messages.

Redundancy: further implications

So what use is redundancy? It performs two main types of functions: the first is technical, and is well defined by Shannon and Weaver; the second involves extending their concept into the social dimension.

Redundancy as a technical aid

Shannon and Weaver show how redundancy helps the accuracy of decoding and provides a check that enables us to identify errors. I can only identify a spelling mistake because of the redundancy in the language. In a non-redundant language, changing a letter would mean changing the word. Thus 'comming' would be a different word from 'coming' and you would not be able to tell that the first word was a misspelling. Of course, the context might help. In so far as it did, the context would be a source of redundancy. In a natural language, words are not equiprobable. If I say 'Spring is . . .' then I am creating a context in which 'coming' is more probable and thus more redundant than, say, 'a pane of glass'. It is, of course, possible that a poet, or even an advertiser for new windows, might write 'Spring is a pane of glass', but that would be a highly entropic use of language.

We are always checking the accuracy of any message we receive against the probable; and what is probable is determined by our experience of the code, context, and type of message – in other words, by our experience of convention and usage. *Convention* is a major source of redundancy, and thus of easy decoding. A writer who breaks with convention does not want to be easily understood: writers who desire easy communication with their readers use appropriate conventions. We will return to this question of convention and redundancy later.

Redundancy also helps overcome the deficiencies of a noisy channel. We repeat ourselves on a bad telephone line; when spelling words on radio or telephone we say A for apple, S for sugar, and so on. An advertiser whose message has to compete with many others for our attention (that is, who has to use a noisy channel) will plan a simple, repetitious, predictable message. One who can expect to have our undivided attention, as, for example, with a technical advertisement in a specialist journal, can design a more entropic message which contains more information.

Increasing redundancy also helps overcome the problems of transmitting an entropic message. A message that is completely unexpected, or that is the opposite of what would be expected, will need saying more than once, often in different ways. Or it may need some special preparation: 'Now, I've got a surprise for you, something you didn't expect at all . . .'.

Redundancy also helps solve problems associated with the audience. If we wish to reach a larger, heterogeneous audience we will need to design a message with a high degree of redundancy. A small, specialist, homogeneous audience, on the other hand, can be reached with a more entropic message. Thus popular art is more redundant than highbrow art. An advertisement for soap powder is more redundant than one for a business computer.

The choice of channel can affect the need for redundancy in the message. Speech needs to be more redundant than writing because the hearer cannot introduce his or her own redundancy as a reader can by reading something twice.

This first function of redundancy, then, is concerned with the way it helps to overcome practical communication problems. These problems may be associated with accuracy and error detection, with the channel and noise, with the nature of the message, or with the audience.

Entropy

Entropy as a concept is of less value for the general student of communication in that it constitutes a communication problem, whereas redundancy is a means of improving communication. But entropy can best be understood as maximum unpredictability. On level A, entropy is simply a measure of the number of choices of signal that can be made and of the randomness of those choices. If I wish to communicate the identities of a pack of playing cards visually by showing all the cards singly, each signal will have maximum entropy if the pack is completely shuffled. If, however, I arrange the cards in order in their suits, each signal will have maximum redundancy, provided that the receiver knows, or can identify, the pattern or structure of a pack of cards.

Redundancy and convention

Structuring a message according to shared patterns, or conventions, is one way of decreasing entropy and increasing redundancy. Imposing an aesthetic pattern or structure on material does precisely the same thing. Rhythmic poetry, by imposing repeatable and therefore predictable patterns of metre and rhyme, decreases entropy and therefore increases redundancy.

Shall I compare thee to a summer's day?
Thou art more lovely and more temperate:
Rough winds do shake the darling buds of . . .

The convention or form of the sonnet has determined that the next word must, on level A, have a single syllable and must rhyme with 'day'. The choice of signal is restricted. Another convention which increases redundancy here is syntax. This reduces the possible choice further – to a noun. On level B, where we expect the word not only to fit the form but also to make sense, we restrict the choice even further. It could not really be 'hay', or 'way'. The word Shakespeare chose, 'May', must in fact be nearly totally redundant. But it feels absolutely right and is aesthetically satisfying. Redundancy is a critical part of the satisfaction provided by the form or structure of a work of art.

The more popular and widely accessible a work of art is, the more it will contain redundancies in form and content. Traditional folk-song or a television series provide obvious examples. Does it therefore follow that highbrow art is necessarily more entropic, in either or both level A (form) and level B (content)? It certainly may do, though communication theory would lead us to conclude that the crucial factor is not the 'level of brow', but the accessibility of the work of art to a wide audience. In other words, there can be popular, highbrow words of art, but these are nearly always conventional – think of Jane Austen or Beethoven as popular highbrows.

When we are dealing with entropy and redundancy in relation to works of art we must remember that we are not dealing with something static and unchanging. An art form or style may break existing conventions, and thus be entropic to its immediate audience, but may then establish its own conventions and thus increase its redundancy as these conventions become learnt and accepted more widely. The way that the Impressionist style of painting was at first rejected by its audience but has now become chocolate-box and calendar cliché is a good example.

Broadly, we may say that encoders, whether artists, preachers, or politicians, who build redundancy into their messages are audience-centred. They care about communicating. Those who do not are more concerned about subject matter, or (if they are artists) form. So redundancy is concerned primarily with the efficiency of communication and the overcoming of communication problems.

Redundancy and social relationships

But I said that there was an extension of this concept that could well perform a different, though related, function. Saying 'Hello' in the street is sending a highly redundant message. But there are no communication problems to solve. There is no noise; I do not wish to put over an entropic content; the audience is receptive. I am engaging in what Jakobson (see below) calls *phatic communication*. By this, he refers to acts of communication that contain nothing new, no information, but that use existing channels simply to keep them open and usable. In fact, of course, there is more to it than that. What I am doing in saying 'Hello' is maintaining and strengthening an existing relationship. Relationships can only exist through constant communication. My 'Hello' may not alter or develop the relationship, but not saying 'Hello' would certainly weaken it.

Social psychologists talk of the ego-drive, a need to have our presence noticed, recognized, and accepted. Not saying 'Hello', that is, cutting someone dead or looking right through them, is frustrating this need. It is socially necessary that I say 'Hello'. Phatic communication, by maintaining and reaffirming relationships, is crucial in holding a community or a society together. And phatic communication is highly redundant; it must be, because it is concerned with existing relationships, not with new information. Conventional behaviour and words in interpersonal situations, such as greetings, are phatic, redundant communication that reaffirms and strengthens social relationships. We call it politeness.

This points to similarities between the two functions of redundancy. The polite person, who indulges in phatic communication, is audience- or receiver-centred in the same way as the communicator who builds redundancy into his or her work. It is no coincidence that the word convention refers to both the behaviour of the polite person and the style of a popular artist.

We can extend this similarity further. A highly conventional art form such as folk-song performs a phatic function. Nothing can be more redundant than the refrain of a folk-song, but in singing it we reaffirm our membership of that particular group or subculture. Indeed, subcultures are often defined partly, if not mainly, by their shared taste in art. Teenage subcultures in our society are identified by the type of music they enjoy or the dance steps they perform. The music or dance is conventional: the shared conventions bind the fans into a subculture. Other forms of music or dance are excluded in so far as they deviate from the accepted conventions. The point is that it is the use of the conventional, redundant aspects of the music or dance that determines and affirms membership of the group. Individual variations are permissible only within the limits of the conventions – or entropic original elements are acceptable only within the redundancy of the form.

Another example of the way that the concept of redundancy enables us to link social behaviour and the form of messages may be seen in the common reception of avant-garde, unconventional, entropic art. The audience is frequently offended or outraged by the way an artist has broken artistic conventions, in just the same way as they would be if the artist had been socially impolite to them. The original reception of the Impressionists or of the early performances of *Waiting for Godot* are obvious instances of this.

If I have dwelt rather longer on redundancy than on other aspects of Shannon and Weaver's model, it is because I find it one of their most fruitful concepts. It does, I believe, offer unique insights into human communication in that it enables us to relate apparently very different elements of the process.

Analysis

Let us test this assertion. Look at plate 1a. Do you find it entropic or redundant? In *form* it is redundant, for it looks like a conventional news

Plate 1a   *'A Mirror of Reality'?*

15

photograph, a moment of hot action caught by the camera. But a closer look at its *content* may give us second thoughts. We do not often see a ring of policemen apparently attacking a respectably dressed young lady (even if she is black). Conventionally, we think of our police as *defenders* of law and order, not as aggressors. Photographs are never as easy to decode as they may appear, and are usually open to a number of readings: one clearly possible reading of this one is that the police are aggressors and the blacks are victims. If this is the message it would be entropic for the typical *Daily Mirror* reader – though probably highly redundant for some urban blacks.

So, when the *Daily Mirror* decided that the dramatic impact of the photo was strong enough to front-page it, they had to do something to decrease the entropy and increase redundancy. In other words, they had to make this image of the police fit more closely with the way we conventionally think of them. Remember that the *Daily Mirror* is a mass-circulation popular newspaper whose stories will therefore be relatively predictable, relatively redundant. So what the editor did was to balance this picture with another one and to surround it with words (plate 1b).

The headlines push our understanding of who were the aggressors and who were the victims back towards the conventional. 'CONFRONTA-TION' suggests that the balance of aggression was at least equal. 'Demo blacks clash with London police' pushes the balance firmly over to the blacks, as does the picture of the injured policeman. The editor has given the original picture a context that makes it fit better into conventional attitudes and beliefs. (In chapter 8, pp. 147ff., I reproduce the results of an audience survey which support this assertion.) He has given it a higher degree of redundancy. We can see both types of redundancy at work here. On the technical level, the context simply makes the picture easier to decode, especially at a quick, first glance. On the level of social relationships we can see it reinforcing social bonds. It shows that we (the readers) are a community who share the same attitudes, the same social meanings. We see things in the same way. This reinforces both our social links with others and our sense of the rightness of our view of the world.

Redundancy is generally a force for the status quo and against change. Entropy is less comfortable, more stimulating, more shocking perhaps, but harder to communicate effectively.

Plate 1b   The *Daily Mirror*

Channel, medium, code

Basic concepts

There are two other important concepts in the model that we have not yet commented on: these are *channel* and *code*. We can really only define them properly in relation to a word that Shannon and Weaver do not use, but that later authorities have found useful. This word is *medium*.

Channel

The channel is the easiest of the three concepts to define. It is simply the physical means by which the signal is transmitted. The main channels are light waves, sound waves, radio waves, telephone cables, the nervous system, and the like.

Medium

The medium is basically the technical or physical means of converting the message into a signal capable of being transmitted along the channel. My voice is a medium; the technology of broadcasting is what constitutes the media of radio and television. The technological or physical properties of a medium are determined by the nature of the channel or channels available for its use. These properties of the medium then determine the range of codes which it can transmit. We can divide media into three main categories.

1. The presentational media: the voice, the face, the body. They use the 'natural' languages of spoken words, expressions, gestures, and so on. They require the presence of the communicator, for he or she is the medium; they are restricted to the here and now, and produce *acts* of communication.
2. The representational media: books, paintings, photographs, writing, architecture, interior decorating, gardening, etc. There are numerous media that use cultural and aesthetic conventions to create a 'text' of some sort. They are representational, creative. They make a text that can record the media of category 1 and that can exist independently of the communicator. They produce *works* of communication.
3. The mechanical media: telephones, radio, television, telexes. They are transmitters of categories 1 and 2. The main distinction between categories 2 and 3 is that the media in 3 use channels created by engineering and are thus subject to greater technological constraints and are more affected by level-A noise than those in category 2.

But the categories do leak into each other and you may find it convenient at times to merge them into one. Categorization involves identifying differences, but it is as important to think of the similarities between media as their differences.

Medium: further implications

A good example of an exploration of media similarities and differences is a study by Katz, Gurevitch, and Hass (1973). They explained the interrelationships of the five main mass media with a circular model (see figure 3). They used a large-scale audience survey to find out why people turned to a particular medium in preference to the others. They investigated the needs that people felt and their reasons for turning to a particular medium to satisfy them. People's responses enabled the researchers to arrange the media in the circular relationship shown in figure 3. The audience felt that each medium was most similar to its two neighbours, or, to put it another way, they felt that if one medium were not available, its functions would be best served by the ones on either side of it.

Figure 3   *Media relationships*

People tended to use newspapers, radio, and television to connect themselves to society, but used books and films to escape from reality for a while. The better-educated tended to use the print media; those with less education were inclined towards the electronic and visual media. Books were the medium most used for improving one's understanding of self.

If we look at the main needs that people use the media to satisfy, and then relate them to people's preferred choice of actual medium to provide that satisfaction, we can produce a table like table 1.

Code: basic concepts

A code is a system of meaning common to the members of a culture or subculture. It consists both of signs (i.e. physical signals that stand for something other than themselves) and of rules or conventions that determine how and in what contexts these signs are used and how they

19

Table 1 *Audience needs*

Needs	Media order of preference for satisfying needs				
	1st	2nd	3rd	4th	5th
A. Personal needs					
1. Understanding self	B	N	R	T	C
2. Enjoyment	C	T	B	R	N
3. Escapism	B	C	T	R	N
B. Social needs					
1. Knowledge about the world	N	R	T	B	C
2. *Self-confidence, stability, self-esteem	N	R	T	B	C
3. Strengthen connections with family	T	C	R	N	B
4. Strengthen connections with friends	C	T	N	R	B

* This need is articulated in three main ways: the need to feel influential and the need to feel that others think in similar ways and hold similar aspirations.
Key: B = books, C = cinema, N = newspapers, R = radio, T = television

can be combined to form more complex messages. The way codes relate to and develop within their parent culture is complex. In chapter 4 we will study codes in some detail. Here I wish to do no more than to define the term, and to consider the basic relationships between codes, channels, and media.

The simplest is between code and *channel*. Clearly the physical characteristics of channels determine the nature of the codes that they can transmit. The telephone is limited to verbal language and paralanguage (the codes of intonation, stress, volume, etc.). We have evolved a number of *secondary codes* simply to make an already encoded message transmittable along a particular channel. A message in the primary code of verbal language may be re-encoded into a variety of secondary codes – morse, semaphore, deaf-and-dumb sign language, handwriting, Braille, printing. All of these secondary codes are determined by the physical properties of their channels, or mechanical media of communication.

The relationship between *medium* and code is not so clear cut. Television is a medium which uses the channels of vision and sound. Buscombe (1975) notes that a programme like *Match of the Day* uses both channel-specific codes and medium-specific codes. The channel-specific codes are:

visual channel – live action, studio shots, and graphics;
aural channel – recorded noises, speech, and music.

He then analyses the medium-specific codes used in the visual channel. These are the codes of lighting, colour, speed, definition, framing, camera movement and placing, and editing. He demonstrates that while the technical constraints of the medium define the range of possible uses open to each code, the actual use made of them is determined by the culture of the broadcasters.

But if we take a medium such as 'dress', for example, we find it difficult to distinguish between the codes and the medium. Is it useful to talk of different codes of dress, or simply of different messages being sent by the same code? The formally agreed meaning of a button or piece of braid on a military uniform differs certainly in degree but not necessarily in kind from the informally agreed less precise meaning of denim jeans. The medium and the code have the same boundaries, but the code is what we need to study, because the code is the significant use to which the medium is put. All cultures and societies have the medium of dress (including nudists, who are defined by its absence): communication occurs through the culturally based codes that the medium conveys.

Dress also has a non-communicative function – that of protection from the elements. Most cultural artefacts have this dual function – a physical, technological one and communication. Houses, cars, furniture are defined first by their technological function and second, through their design, by their communicative function. The constraints of the medium are technological: the codes operate within them.

Feedback

Basic concepts

Like medium, *feedback* is a concept that Shannon and Weaver do not use, but is one that later workers have found useful. Briefly, feedback is the transmission of the receiver's reaction back to the sender. Models that emphasize feedback are ones with a cybernetic bias.

Cybernetics is the science of control. The word derives from the Greek word for helmsman and its origin can provide us with a good illustration. If a helmsman wishes to steer to port, he moves the tiller to starboard. He then watches to see how far the ship's bow will swing round to port and will adjust the extent to which he pushes the tiller to starboard accordingly. His eyes enable him to receive the feedback – that is, the response of the bow to his initial movement of the tiller. In the same way, the thermostat in a central-heating system sends messages to the boiler, and receives messages from the thermometer measuring the room temperature. This feedback enables it to adjust the performance of the boiler to the needs of the room. The same is true in human communication. Feedback enables the speaker to adjust his or her performance to the needs and responses of an audience. Good speakers are generally sensitive to feedback; pompous, domineering bores manage to filter out feedback almost entirely.

Some channels of communication make feedback very difficult. Two-way radios and telephones allow alternating transmission which can perform some of the functions of feedback, but the feedback is clearly of a different order from the simultaneous feedback that occurs during face-to-face communication. This is determined mainly by availability of channels. In face-to-face communication I can transmit with my voice and simultaneously receive with my eyes. Another factor is access to these channels. The mechanical media, particularly the mass media, limit access and therefore limit feedback. We cannot have constant access to the BBC, though its audience research unit tries to provide the Corporation with a formalized system of feedback. In the same way, when I am giving a lecture, my students' access to the channel of sound waves is limited – they give me less feedback than in a seminar, where they have a far greater share of the speaking time.

Feedback, then, has this one main function. It helps the communicator adjust his or her message to the needs and responses of the receiver. It also has a number of subsidiary functions. Perhaps the most important of these is that it helps the receiver to feel involved in the communication. Being aware that the communicator is taking account of our response makes us more likely to accept the message: being unable to express our response can lead to a build-up of frustration that can cause so much noise that the message may become totally lost. Though feedback inserts a return loop from destination to source, it does not destroy the linearity of the model. It is there to make the process of transmitting messages more efficient.

Suggestions for further work

1. Apply Shannon and Weaver's levels A, B, and C to the analysis of different examples of communication, e.g. a job interview, a news photograph, a pop song. How widely are they applicable? How useful do you find this sort of analytical exercise?

2. What are the problems of taking the concept of 'information' which originated in level A and referring it to level B? Can meaning be numerically measured? See Smith (1966), pp. 15–24, 41–55 and Cherry (1957), pp. 169–78, 182–9, 228–34, 243–52.
3. What do we mean by saying that the English language is 50 per cent redundant? See Cherry (1957), pp. 117–23, 182–9 and Smith (1966), p. 21.
4. Outline the main communicative functions of redundancy. See also Cherry (1957), pp. 278–9.
5. Discuss the ways in which convention can be said to facilitate understanding. Collect examples of writers/artists who either break or extend specific conventions. How does this affect their desire to communicate or the audience that they reach?
6. Consider a book, a photograph, a record, a live play and a filmed version of it. How can we categorize them as media? See Guiraud (1975), pp. 15–21.
7. Take a number of examples of media and channels. Clearly one medium can use more than one channel and one channel can convey more than one medium: is there therefore any significant relationship between medium and channel or are they independent concepts?

2 OTHER MODELS

In this chapter I intend to take a number of other process models of communication in order to illustrate the range of this approach. The first, Gerbner's, is like Shannon and Weaver's in that it claims to be universally applicable: it can explain any example of communication, and in particular draws attention to those key elements that are common to each and every act of communication. We shall then look at some models with more specific and limited claims. Lasswell takes the basic shape of Shannon and Weaver's model, verbalizes it, and then applies it specifically to the mass media. Newcomb breaks with this approach by giving us a new triangular shape for a model, and by referring it mainly to interpersonal or social communication. Westley and MacLean bring this model back towards the more familiar linear shape when they develop it for application to the mass media. Finally we look at Jakobson's model, which can be seen as a bridge between the process and semiotic models of communication.

Gerbner's model (1956)

George Gerbner, now Professor and Head of the Annenberg School of Communications, in the University of Pennsylvania, produced an attempt at a general-purpose model of communication. It was considerably more complex than Shannon and Weaver's but still took their linear process model as its skeleton. The main advances over their model, however, are two: it relates the message to the 'reality' that it is 'about' and thus enables us to approach questions of perception and meaning, and it sees the communication process as consisting of two alternating dimensions –

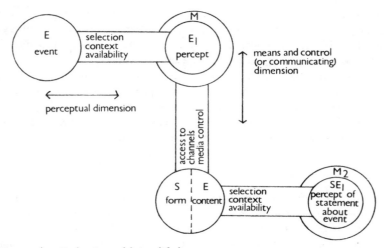

Figure 4   *Gerbner's model (modified)*

the perceptual or receptive, and the communicating or means and control dimension. The main elements of Gerbner's model are shown in figure 4.

Horizontal dimension

The process begins with an event E, something in external reality which is perceived by M (and M can be a human or a machine such as a camera or a microphone). M's perception of E is a percept E_1. This is the perceptual dimension at the start of the process. The relationship between E and E_1 involves selection, in that M cannot possibly perceive the whole complexity of E. If M is a machine, the selection is determined by its engineering, its physical capacities. If M is a human, however, the selection is more complex. Human perception is not a simple reception of stimuli, but is a process of interaction or negotiation. What happens is that we try to match the external stimuli with internal patterns of thought or concepts. When this match has been made, we have perceived something, we have given it meaning. So 'meaning' in this sense derives from the matching of external stimuli with internal concepts. Consider what happens if we fail to hear a word clearly, or cannot decipher someone's handwriting. Or think of the visual puzzles of photographs of familiar objects taken from unfamiliar angles or in unfamiliar close up; once the matching or recognition has occurred, the photograph is easily perceived for what it is. Until this moment, we are in a state of frustration, for, although we can see the tones and shapes of the photograph, we cannot say we perceive it yet, for perception always involves the drive to understand and organize. Failing to see meaning in what we perceive puts us into a state of disorientation.

This matching is controlled by our culture, in that our internal concepts or patterns of thought have developed as a result of our cultural experience. This means that people of different cultures will perceive reality differently. Perception, then, is not just a psychological process within the individual; it is also a matter of culture.

Vertical dimension

We now move to the second stage and into the vertical dimension. This is when the percept E_1 is converted into a signal about E, or to use Gerbner's code, SE. This is what we normally call a message, that is a signal or statement about the event. The circle representing this message is divided into two; S refers to it as a signal, the form that it takes, and E refers to its content. It is clear that a given content or E can be communicated in a number of different ways — there are a number of potential Ss to choose from. Finding the best S for the given E is one of the crucial concerns of the communicator. It is important to remember that SE is a unified concept, not two separate areas brought together, in that the chosen S will obviously affect the presentation of E — the relationship between form and content is dynamic and interactive. Content is not simply conveyed by form, as in what I. A. Richards disparagingly calls the 'vulgar packaging theory of communication'.

Richards uses this colourful phrase to pour scorn on communication theory. For him, Shannon and Weaver's model implies that there is a core message that exists independently. This is then encoded; that is, it is wrapped up in language like a parcel for transmission. The receiver decodes it, or unwraps the packaging and reveals the core message. The fallacy for him is the idea that a message can exist before it is articulated, or 'encoded'. Articulation is a creative process: before it there exists only the drive, the need to articulate, not a pre-existing idea or content that then has to be encoded. In other words, there is no content before form, and the attempt to find a difference between form and content is in itself a very doubtful exercise.

In this vertical or communicating dimension, selection is as important as it is in the horizontal. First there is the selection of the 'means' — the medium and channel of communication. Then there is selection from within the percept E_1. Just as E_1 can never be a complete and comprehensive response to E, so too a signal about E_1 can never in its turn attain completeness or comprehensiveness. Selection and distortion must occur.

Access: basic concept

This dimension also contains the concept of access to the media and channels of communication. Who has access to the mass media in particular is currently a burning issue in the debate on the relationship of television and society. The horizontal dimension of this model tells us that television's E_1 must be a selection of E, so who makes the selection and whose picture of the world is transmitted as SE is obviously of prime importance. Trade unions claim, with some justification, that in its handling of industrial news, television always presents a middle-class, management-inclined version. This is not necessarily deliberate, but may be explained by the fact that television personnel are normally closer in class, culture, and educational background to the managers than they are to the workers, and therefore their E_1 will naturally involve the same sort of selection of E as would the managers'.

Access: further implications

Access to the media is a means of exerting power and social control. This is widely believed of the mass media: to find illustrations we have only to look at the relationship between authoritarian governments or dictators and their media, or to see how one of the first targets of successful revolutionary forces is the national radio station. But it is also true in interpersonal communication: authoritarian personalities or teachers will attempt to control the access of others to the channels of communication: that is, they will attempt to limit the amount that others talk. The Victorian father not allowing his children to speak unless spoken to at the dinner table was acting in precisely the same way as the modern totalitarian government allowing only 'official' versions of events on its television screens.

The question of the similarity between democracy and access to the mass media, and type of human relationship and access to the interpersonal channels can be a stimulating one to explore further.

For the third stage of the process, then, we revert to the horizontal dimension. But here, of course, what is being perceived by the receiver, M_2, is not an event E, but a signal or statement about an event, or SE. The same processes as we outlined in stage 1 are involved and it is perhaps worth re-emphasizing here that the meaning of the message is not 'contained' in the message itself, but is the result of an interaction or negotiation between the receiver and the message. M_2 brings to SE a set of needs and concepts derived from his or her culture or subculture and in so far as s/he can relate SE to them so, we can say, s/he finds meaning in the message. The message itself should be seen as a potential of many meanings. This potential is never completely realized and the form it takes is not determined until interaction or negotiation occurs between M_2 and SE: the resulting meaning is SE_1.

Availability: basic concept

A factor in the horizontal dimension that is the equivalent of 'access' in the vertical is that of 'availability'. Like selectivity, it helps to determine what is actually perceived. It is another form of selectivity, but in this case the selection is not performed by the perceiver but by the communicator. What the communicator selects is how, and therefore to whom, the message is to be made available. An example at the interpersonal level would be when parents use long words, or sometimes spell words out when talking in front of their young children about something they do not wish them to understand. The television company's policy of confining programmes containing sex and violence to after 9.00 p.m. is a way of limiting their availability as was the Soviet government's policy of publishing certain books with very small print runs, so that they would be available only in major libraries, and thus to a restricted readership.

Availability: further implications

Perhaps the most significant increase in availability has been the result of the development of broadcasting. Before radio, access to information was confined to the literate. The ability to read had been necessarily and traditionally confined to the educated minority, who thus controlled the flow of information to the uneducated majority. Information, as we have seen, is power, and thus literacy was a vital way of exerting social control. The spread of universal education was accompanied by widespread fears about 'educating the working classes out of their natural place in society' or 'giving them ideas above their station'. The early socialists and trade unionists saw the education of the workers, particularly the improvement of literacy, as a necessary base for the development of a socialist society. Even today, when education is universal in our society, and literacy almost so, it is still the educated middle classes who turn naturally to the written word to learn new information. It is these classes who value the power of the written word to stimulate thought and imagination and who most use its ability to offer escapism and relaxation.

Radio and television, and to a lesser extent the cinema, have, for the first time in our history, made information directly available to the non-literate, and thus are potentially major agents of democracy. Radio is particularly important in this, for cheapness of both the transmitters and receivers widens its availability. The desire of developing countries to control their radio output is significant, for the democratizing potential of radio is directly linked to the access allowed to it. Third World governments who control access to their mass media often argue that their politically unsophisticated people cannot handle the flow of frequently contradictory information that results from the freer access to the media in western democracies. Access and availability are two sides of the same coin.

The model extended

The model allows multiple extensions, and enables us to include human and mechanical agents in the process. For instance, Gerbner models a telephone conversation and, at the same time, illustrates his model's basic similarity to Shannon and Weaver's (see figure 5).

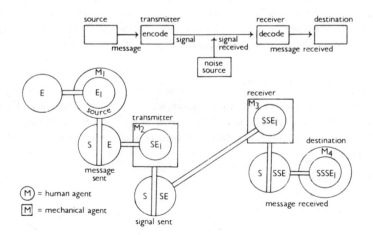

Figure 5   *Comparison between Shannon and Weaver's model (top) and Gerbner's (bottom)*

Model and meaning

Gerbner's basic model is the triangular relationship between event E, percept of event E_1, and statement about event SE. Meaning is to be found primarily in this relationship: indeed, in one later variant of his model Gerbner links E to SE with an arrow labelled 'truth quality'. But his extension of his model to include M_3, the receiver, does allow us to add the receiver's percept of the message to these factors that determine the meaning.

But, for all its elaboration, Gerbner's model is still just an imaginative development of that of Shannon and Weaver. It defines communication as the transmission of messages, and although it looks beyond the process itself, outside to E, and thus raises the question of meaning, it never addresses itself directly to the problems of how meaning is generated. It takes S, the form of the message or the codes used, for granted, whereas the proponents of the semiotic school would find this the heart of the matter. They would also argue that Gerbner is wrong to assume that all the horizontal processes are similar: our perception of a message is not the same as our perception of an event. We do not respond to a film of the villain being gunned down by the hero in the same way as we would if we were witnesses to the real-life event. A message is structured or encoded in a way that a raw event is not, and thus it directs our response more actively.

Gerbner's later work, particularly his studies on the portrayal of violence on television, shows that he is aware of these deficiencies in his model, and indeed Gerbner is the one major authority whose work comes closest to combining the two approaches to the study of communication.

Lasswell's model (1948)

Lasswell has given us another widely quoted early model. His, though, is specifically one of mass communication. He argues that to understand the processes of mass communication we need to study each of the stages in his model:

> *Who*
> Says *what*
> In *which channel*
> To *whom*
> With *what effect?*

This is a verbal version of Shannon and Weaver's original model. It is still linear: it sees communication as the transmission of messages: it raises the issue of 'effect' rather than meaning. 'Effect' implies an observable and measurable change in the receiver that is caused by identifiable elements in the process. Changing one of these elements will change the effect: we can change the encoder, we can change the message, we can change the channel: each one of these changes should produce the appropriate change in the effect. Most mass-communication research has implicitly followed this model. The work on institutions and their processes, on the producers of communication, on the audience and how it is affected, clearly derives from a process-based linear model.

Newcomb's model (1953)

But not all of these models are linear. Newcomb's is one that introduces us to a fundamentally different shape. It is triangular (see figure 6). Its main significance, however, lies in the fact that it is the first of our models to introduce the role of communication in a society or a social relationship. For Newcomb this role is simple – it is to maintain equilibrium within the social system. The way the model works is this. A and B are communicator and receiver; they may be individuals, or management and union, or government and people. X is part of their social environment. ABX is a system, which means that its internal relations are interdependent: if A changes, B and X will change as well; or if A changes her or his relationship to X, B will have to change his or her relationship either with X or with A.

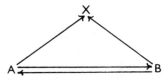

Figure 6   *Schematic illustration of the minimal ABX system*

Notes
The minimal components of the ABX system are as follows:
1. A's orientation towards X, including both attitude towards X as an object to be approached or avoided (characterized by sign and intensity) and cognitive attributes (beliefs and cognitive structuring).
2. A's orientation towards B, in exactly the same sense. (To avoid confusing terms, we shall speak of positive and negative *attraction* towards A or B as persons, and of favourable and unfavourable *attitudes* towards X.)
3. B's orientation towards X.
4. B's orientation towards A.

If A and B are friends, and X is something or someone known to both of them, it will be important that A and B have similar attitudes to X. If they do, the system will be in equilibrium. But if A likes X and B does not, then A and B will be under pressure to communicate until the two friends arrive at broadly similar attitudes to X. The more important a place X has in their social environment, the more urgent will be their drive to share an orientation towards him or it. Of course, X may not be a thing or a person: it may be any part of their shared environment. A may be the government, B the TUC, and X pay policy: in this case we can see, to oversimplify for the sake of clarity, that a Labour government (A) and the TUC (B), who in theory 'like' each other, will be under pressure to hold frequent meetings to try and agree on X, the pay policy. But if A is a Tory government who is not 'friends' with B, the TUC, there will be less pressure for them to agree on X. If the AB relationship is not one of 'liking' they can differ over X: the system is still in equilibrium.

Another example of the way equilibrium increases the need to communicate can be seen when X changes. Immediately A and B need to communicate to establish their co-orientation to the new X. I took part in a small study of people's reactions to the news of Harold Wilson's resignation as Prime Minister. Their normal reaction was immediately to talk about it to find out what their friends thought, so that they could quickly arrive at a common orientation towards his successor. In time of war, people's dependence on the media is increased, and so too is the government's use of the media. This is because the war, X, is not only of crucial importance but is also constantly changing. So government and people (A and B) need to be in constant communication via the mass media.

This model assumes, though does not explicitly state, that people need information. In a democracy information is usually regarded as a right, but it is not always realized that information is also a necessity. Without it we cannot feel part of a society. We must have adequate information about our social environment in order both to know how to react to it and to identify in our reaction factors that we can share with the fellow members of our peer group, subculture, or culture.

Westley and MacLean's model (1957)

This social need for information underlies Westley and MacLean's extension of Newcomb's model (see figures 7 and 8). They adopt it specifically for the mass media. The root of this is clearly Newcomb's

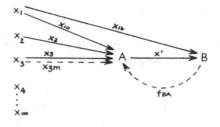

Figure 7   *The basic communication model*

Note

The Xs are selected and abstracted by communicator A and transmitted as a message (X') to B, who may or may not have part or all of the Xs in his or her own sensory field (X_{1b}). Either purposively or non-purposively B transmits feedback (f_{BA}) to A.

ABX, but Westley and MacLean have made two fundamental changes. They have introduced a new element, C, which is the editorial-communicating function: that is, it is the process of deciding what and how to communicate. They have also started to stretch the model so that it is beginning to return to the familiar linear shape of the process-centred models with which we started. X is now nearer A than B, and the arrows are one-way. A is becoming closer to the encoder of Shannon and Weaver, and C has some elements of the transmitter. The fragmentation of X to show its multifarious nature is a less significant, but useful, modification. When Westley and MacLean apply their model specifically to mass communication they stretch it even further away from Newcomb's triangle (see figure 9). A may be seen as the reporter who sends in a story

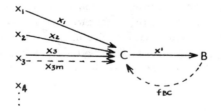

Figure 8   *The addition of an editorial function*

Note

What Xs B receives may be owing to selected abstractions transmitted by a non-purposive encoder (C), acting for B and thus extending B's environment. C's selections are necessarily based in part on feedback (F_{BC}) from B.

33

to C, his or her paper/radio/television newsroom. The editorial and publishing/broadcasting process (which are contained within C) then work on and transmit this story to B, the audience. In this model B has lost any direct or immediate experience of X, as he or she has lost a direct relationship with A.

Westley and MacLean claim that the mass media extend the social environment to which B needs to relate and also provide the means by which that relationship or orientation is performed. They maintain Newcomb's idea that the need to maintain a shared orientation towards X is a motive for communication, and they allow for restricted opportunities for feedback. But they have crucially shifted the balance of Newcomb's system. A and C now play dominant roles. B is very much at their mercy. The mass society in which we live has inevitably enlarged the social environment to which we need to orientate ourselves. So B's need for information and orientation has increased, but the means of satisfying this need have been restricted: the mass media are the only means available. He or she becomes, in the logical extension of this model, totally dependent upon the mass media.

This dependency model fails to take account of the relationship between the mass media and the other means we have of orientating ourselves to our social environment: these include the family, work mates, friends, school, the church, trade unions, and all the other formal and informal networks of relationships through which we fit into our society. We are not as dependent upon the media as this model implies.

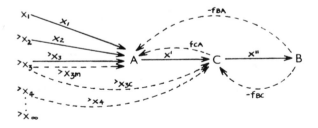

Figure 9   *The mass-communication model*

Note

The messages C transmits to B (X'') represent his selections from both messages to him from A's (X') and C's selections and abstractions from Xs in his own sensory field (X$_{3C}$, X$_4$), which may or may not be Xs in A's field. Feedback not only moves from B to A (f$_{BA}$) and from B to C (f$_{BC}$) but also from C to A (f$_{CA}$).

Jakobson's model (1960)

Jakobson's has similarities with both the linear and the triangular models. But he is a linguist, and as such is interested in matters like meaning and the internal structure of the message. He thus bridges the gap between the process and semiotic schools. His model is a double one. He starts by modelling the *constitutive factors* in an act of communication. These are the six factors that must be present for communication to be possible. He then models the functions that this act of communication performs for each factor.

He starts on a familiar linear base. An *addresser* sends a *message* to an *addressee*. He recognizes that this message must refer to something other than itself. This he calls the *context*: this gives the third point of the triangle whose other two points are the addresser and the addressee. So far, so familiar. He then adds two other factors: one is *contact*, by which he means the physical channel and psychological connections between the addresser and the addressee; the other, final factor is a *code*, a shared meaning system by which the message is structured. He visualizes his model as figure 10.

	Context	
Addresser	Message	Addressee
	- - - - -	
	Contact	
	Code	

Figure 10   *The constitutive factors of communication*

Each of these factors, he argues, determines a different function of language, and in each act of communication we can find a hierarchy of functions. Jakobson produces an identically structured model to explain the six functions (each function occupies the same place in the model as the factor to which it refers). This is shown in figure 11.

The *emotive* function describes the relationship of the message to the addresser: we often use the word 'expressive' to refer to it. The message's emotive function is to communicate the addresser's emotions, attitudes,

	Referential	
Emotive	Poetic	Conative
	Phatic	
	Metalingual	

Figure 11   *The functions of communication*

status, class; all those elements that make the message uniquely personal. In some messages, such as love poetry, this emotive function is paramount. In others, such as news reporting, it is repressed. At the other end of the process is the *conative* function. This refers to the effect of the message on the addressee. In commands or propaganda, this function assumes paramount importance; in other types of communication it is relegated to a lower priority. The *referential* function, the 'reality orientation' of the message, is clearly of top priority in objective, factual communication. This is communication that is concerned to be 'true' or factually accurate. These three are obvious, common-sense functions, performed in varying degrees by all acts of communication, and they correspond fairly closely to the A, B, and X of Newcomb.

The next three functions may appear less familiar at first sight, though one of them, the phatic, has been discussed in different terms already. The *phatic* function is to keep the channels of communication open; it is to maintain the relationship between addresser and addressee: it is to confirm that communication is taking place. It is thus orientated towards the contact factor, the physical and psychological connections that must exist. It is performed, in other words, by the *redundant* element of messages. The second function of redundancy (see pp. 10ff.) is phatic.

The *metalingual* function is that of identifying the code that is being used. When I use the word 'redundancy' I may need to make explicit the fact that I am using the code of communication theory and not that of employment. An empty cigarette packet thrown down on an old piece of newspaper is normally litter. But if the packet is stuck to the paper, the whole mounted in a frame and hung on the wall of an art gallery, it becomes art. The frame performs the metalingual function of saying 'Decode this according to fine-art meanings': it invites us to look for aesthetic proportions and relationships, to see it as a metaphor for the 'throw-away society', people as litter-makers. All messages have to have an explicit or implicit metalingual function. They have to identify the code they are using in some way or other.

The final function is the *poetic*. This is the relationship of the message to itself. In aesthetic communication, this is clearly central; in the example above, the metalingual function of the frame necessarily emphasizes the poetic function of the aesthetic relationship between cigarette packet and newspaper. But Jakobson points out that this function operates in ordinary conversation as well. We say 'innocent bystander' rather than 'uninvolved onlooker' because its rhythmic pattern is more aesthetically pleasing. Jakobson uses the political slogan 'I like Ike' to illustrate the poetic function. It consists of three monosyllables, each with the diphthong 'ay'. Two of them rhyme. They use only two consonants. And it all adds up to a poetically pleasing and therefore memorable slogan. But we can take this analysis further. Let us imagine the slogan as a lapel badge.

Metalingually we must identify it as using the code of political communication. The wearer does not know General Eisenhower or like

him personally. 'Like' in this case means 'support politically'. So too 'Ike' means not just the individual man, but the political party whose candidate he is and whose policies he represents. In another code, that of personal relationships, 'I like Ike' would have very different meanings.

Emotively this tells us about the addresser, his political position and how strongly he feels about it. *Conatively*, its function will be to persuade the addressee to support the same political programme, to agree with the addresser. Its *referential* function is to refer to an existing man and programme, to make the addressee think of what he already knows of General Eisenhower and his policies. Finally, its *phatic* function is to identify membership of the group of Eisenhower supporters, to maintain and strengthen the fellow-feeling that exists among its members.

Models and modelling

We have looked at a selection of models that see communication as a process. There are, of course, many more. But the ones we have studied illustrate the nature and purpose of modelling. A model is like a map. It represents selected features of its territory: no map or model can be comprehensive. A road map highlights different features from a map of the climate or the geology of a country. This means that we have to be purposeful and deliberate in our choice of map; we have to know *why* we have turned to it and what insights we require from it.

The trouble with models is that their purposes are usually less well signalled. In fact, many claim a comprehensiveness that can never be achieved. But the value of a model is that (a) it highlights systematically selected features of its territory, (b) it points to selected interrelationships between these features, and (c) the system behind the selection in (a) and (b) provides a definition and delineation of the territory being modelled. Modelling is useful and necessary, particularly as a basis for structuring a programme of study or research. But we must remember its limitations. McKeown (1982) discusses modelling in more detail.

Suggestions for further work

1. Discuss ways in which access to the media relates to social control. Your discussion should refer both to the mass media and to the interpersonal media.

2. Compare fully Gerbner's vertical and horizontal dimensions. Use his model to analyse a piece of communication (for example a family discussion on a television newscast or a classroom lesson). What aspects of communication does he highlight most effectively? See, for questions 1 and 2, McQuail (1975) and/or Corner and Hawthorn (1980), pp. 26–7.

3. Newcomb's model posited an equilibrium within the ABX system. Do you consider that Westley and MacLean's additions/modifications have destroyed this equilibrium and thus the main point of Newcomb's model? Does the fact that Newcomb's model is designed to explain interpersonal communication whereas Westley and MacLean's is designed for mass communication adequately account for the differences between the two? See Smith (1966), pp. 66–79, 80–7 and McQuail (1975), pp. 19–27.

4. Explore the similarities and differences between Jakobson's six functions, Newcomb's ABX, Gerbner's E, E_1, and M, and redundancy. See Hawkes (1977), pp. 83–7 and Guiraud (1975), pp. 5–9 for Jakobson's model.

5. How much can any of the models discussed in these two chapters explain or help us to understand works of art? Do, or should, works of art communicate in the way that these models explain communication? See McKeown (1982).

6. Turn to plate 4 (pp. 54–5). Use Jakobson's model to analyse the communicative functions of a selection of the images. Use a bar chart to indicate the relative priority of the different functions, e.g. for images d, l, and e. Do you agree with the way I have analysed them in the chart below? I found the phatic and metalingual functions the hardest to express graphically. Is this your experience? If so, can you offer an explanation for it?

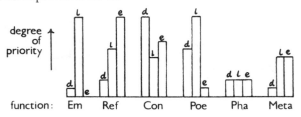

3 COMMUNICATION, MEANING, AND SIGNS

The models we have considered so far have all, in varying degrees, emphasized the *process* of communication. They assume basically that communication is the transfer of a message from A to B. Consequently, their main concerns are with medium, channel, transmitter, receiver, noise, and feedback, for these are all terms relating to this process of sending a message. We now turn our attention to a radically different approach to the study of communication. Here the emphasis is not so much on communication as a process, but on communication as the generation of meaning. When I communicate with you, you understand, more or less accurately, what my message means. For communication to take place I have to create a message out of signs. This message stimulates you to create a meaning for yourself that relates in some way to the meaning that I generated in my message in the first place. The more we share the same codes, the more we use the same sign systems, the closer our two 'meanings' of the message will approximate to each other.

This places a different emphasis on the study of communication, and we will have to familiarize ourselves with a new set of terms. These are terms like sign, signification, icons, index, denote, connote – all terms which refer to various ways of creating meaning. So these models will differ from the ones just discussed in that they are not linear: they do not contain arrows indicating the flow of the message. They are *structural* models, and any arrows indicate *relationships* between elements in this creation of meaning. These models do not assume a series of steps or stages through which a message passes: rather they concentrate on analysing a structured set of relationships which enable a message to signify something; in other words, they concentrate on what it is that makes marks on paper or sounds in the air into a *message*.

Semiotics

At the centre of this concern is the sign. The study of signs and the way they work is called semiotics or semiology, and this will provide the alternative focus in this book. Semiotics, as we will call it, has three main areas of study:

1. The sign itself. This consists of the study of different varieties of signs, of the different ways they have of conveying meaning, and of the way they relate to the people who use them. For signs are human constructs and can only be understood in terms of the uses people put them to.
2. The codes or systems into which signs are organized. This study covers the ways that a variety of codes have developed in order to meet the needs of a society or culture, or to exploit the channels of communication available for their transmission.
3. The culture within which these codes and signs operate. This in turn is dependent upon the use of these codes and signs for its own existence and form.

Semiotics, then, focuses its attention primarily on the text. The linear, process models give the text no more attention than any other stage in the process: indeed, some of them pass it over almost without comment. This is one major difference between the two approaches. The other is the status of the receiver. In semiotics, the receiver, or reader, is seen as playing a more active role than in most of the process models (Gerbner's is an exception). Semiotics prefers the term 'reader' (even of a photograph of a painting) to 'receiver' because it implies both a greater degree of activity and also that reading is something we learn to do; it is thus determined by the cultural experience of the reader. The reader helps to create the meaning of the text by bringing to it his or her experience, attitudes, and emotions.

In this chapter I wish to start by looking at some of the main approaches to this complex question of meaning. I shall then go on to consider the role played by signs in generating this meaning, and to categorize signs into different types according to their different ways of performing this function.

Signs and meaning

Basic concepts

All the models of meaning share a broadly similar form. Each is concerned with three elements which must be involved in some way or other in any study of meaning. These are: (1) the sign, (2) that to which it refers, and (3) the users of the sign.

A sign is something physical, perceivable by our senses; it refers to something other than itself; and it depends upon a recognition by its users that it *is* a sign. Take our earlier example: pulling my earlobe as a sign to an auctioneer. In this case the sign refers to my bid, and this is recognized as such by both the auctioneer and myself. Meaning is conveyed from me to the auctioneer: communication has taken place.

In this chapter we shall study the two most influential models of meaning. The first is that of the philosopher and logician C. S. Peirce (we will also look at the variant of Ogden and Richards), and the second is that of the linguist Ferdinand de Saussure.

Peirce (and Ogden and Richards) see the sign, that to which it refers, and its users as the three points of a triangle. Each is closely related to the other two, and can be understood only in terms of the others. Saussure takes a slightly different line. He says that the sign consists of its physical form plus an associated mental concept, and that this concept is in its turn an apprehension of external reality. The sign relates to reality only through the concepts of the people who use it.

Thus the word CAR (marks on paper or sounds in air) has a mental concept attached to it. Mine will be broadly the same as yours, though there may be some individual differences. This shared concept then relates to a class of objects in reality. This is so straightforward as to seem obvious, but there can be problems. My wife and I, for example, frequently argue over whether something is blue or green. We share the same language, we are looking at the same piece of external reality: the difference lies in the concepts of blueness or greenness that link our words to that reality.

Further implications

C. S. Peirce

Peirce (1931–58) and Ogden and Richards (1923) arrived at very similar models of how signs signify. Both identified a triangular relationship

41

between the sign, the user, and external reality as a necessary model for studying meaning. Peirce, who is commonly regarded as the founder of the American tradition of semiotics, explained his model simply:

> A sign is something which stands to somebody for something in some respect or capacity. It addresses somebody, that is, creates in the mind of that person an equivalent sign, or perhaps a more developed sign. The sign which it creates I call the *interpretant* of the first sign. The sign stands for something, *its object*. (In Zeman, 1977)

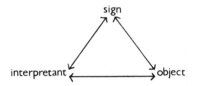

Figure 12   *Peirce's elements of meaning*

Peirce's three terms can be modelled as in figure 12. The double-ended arrows emphasize that each term can be understood only in relation to the others. A *sign* refers to something other than itself – the *object*, and is understood by somebody: that is, it has an effect in the mind of the user – the *interpretant*. We must realize that the interpretant is not the user of the sign, but what Peirce calls elsewhere 'the proper significate effect': that is, it is a mental concept produced both by the sign and by the user's experience of the object. The interpretant of the word (sign) SCHOOL in any one context will be the result of the user's experience of that word (s/he would not apply it to a technical college), and of his or her experience of institutions called 'schools', the object. Thus it is not fixed, defined by a dictionary, but may vary within limits according to the experience of the user. The limits are set by social convention (in this case the conventions of the English language); the variation within them allows for the social and psychological differences between the users.

One additional difference between the semiotic and the process models is relevant here. This is that the semiotic models make no distinction between encoder and decoder. The interpretant is the mental concept of the user of the sign, whether this user be speaker or listener, writer or reader, painter or viewer. Decoding is as active and creative as encoding.

Ogden and Richards (1923)

Ogden and Richards were British workers in this area who corresponded regularly with Peirce. They derived a very similar triangular model of meaning. Their referent corresponds closely to Peirce's object, their reference to his interpretant, and their symbol to his sign. In their model, referent and reference are directly connected; so too are symbol and reference. But the connection between symbol and referent is indirect or imputed. This shift away from the equilateral relationship of Peirce's model brings Ogden and Richards closer to Saussure (see below). He, too, relegated the relationship of the sign with external reality to one of minimal importance. Like Saussure, Ogden and Richards put the symbol in the key position: our symbols direct and organize our thoughts or references; and our references organize our perception of reality. Symbol and reference in Ogden and Richards are similar to the signifier and signified in Saussure.

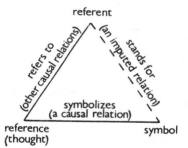

Figure 13   *Ogden and Richards's elements of meaning*

Saussure

If the American logician and philosopher C. S. Peirce was one of the founders of semiotics, the other was undoubtedly the Swiss linguist Ferdinand de Saussure. Peirce's concern as a philosopher was with our understanding of our experience and of the world around us. It was only gradually that he came to realize the importance of *semiotics*, the act of signifying, in this. His interest was in meaning, which he found in the structural relationship of signs, people, and objects.

Saussure, as a linguist, was primarily interested in language. He was more concerned with the way signs (or, in his case, words) related to other signs than he was with the way they related to Peirce's 'object'. So Saussure's basic model differs in emphasis from Peirce's. He focuses his attention much more directly on the sign itself. The sign, for Saussure, was a physical object with a meaning; or, to use his terms, a sign consisted of a *signifier* and a *signified*. The signifier is the sign's image as we perceive it – the marks on the paper or the sounds in the air; the signified is the mental concept to which it refers. This mental concept is broadly common to all members of the same culture who share the same language.

We can see immediately similarities between Saussure's signifier and Peirce's sign, and Saussure's signified and Peirce's interpretant. Saussure, however, is less concerned than Peirce with the relationship of those two elements with Peirce's 'object' or external meaning. When Saussure does turn to this he calls it *signification* but spends comparatively little time on it. So Saussure's model may be visualized as in figure 14.

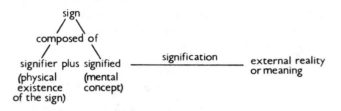

Figure 14 *Saussure's elements of meaning*

For illustration, I might make two marks on the paper, thus:

O X

These might be the first two moves in a game of noughts and crosses (or tick-tack-toe), in which case they remain as mere marks on the paper. Or they might be read as a word, in which case they become a sign composed of the signifier (their appearance) and the mental concept (oxness) which we have of this particular type of animal. The relationship between my concept of oxness and the physical reality of oxen is 'signification': it is my way of giving meaning to the world, of understanding it.

I stress this, because it is important to remember that the signifieds are as much a product of a particular culture as are the signifiers. It is obvious that words, the signifiers, change from language to language. But it is easy to fall into the fallacy of believing that the signifieds are universal and that translation is therefore a simple matter of substituting a French word, say, for an English one – the 'meaning' is the same. This is not so. My mental concept of oxness must be very different from that of an Indian farmer, and teaching me the sound of the Hindu word (signifier) for ox does not get me any nearer to sharing his concept of 'oxness'. The signification of an ox is as culture-specific as is the linguistic form of the signifier in each language.

Sign and system

The deceptively simple question is 'What is an ox?', or, to put it more linguistically or semiotically, 'What do we mean by the sign *ox?*' For Saussure the question can be answered only in the light of what we do *not* mean by that sign.

This is a new approach to the question of how signs signify. The similarity between Saussure and Peirce here is that they both seek meaning in structural relationships, but Saussure considers a new relationship — that between the sign and other signs in the same system: that is, the relationship between a sign and other signs that it could conceivably be, but is not. Thus the meaning of the sign *man* is determined by how it is differentiated from other signs. So *man* can mean *not animal* or *not human* or *not boy* or *not master*.

When Chanel chose the French star Catherine Deneuve to give their perfume an image of a particular kind of sophisticated traditional French chic, she became a sign in a system. And the meaning of Catherine-Deneuve-as-sign was determined by other beautiful stars-as-signs that she was not. She was not Susan Hampshire (too English); she was not Twiggy (too young, trendy, *changeably* fashionable); she was not Brigitte Bardot (too unsophisticatedly sexy); and so on.

According to this model of meaning, the signifieds are the mental concepts we use to divide reality up and categorize it so that we can understand it. The boundaries between one category and another are artificial, not natural, for nature is all of a piece. There is no line between man and boy until we draw one, and scientists are constantly trying to define more accurately the boundary between humans and other animals. So signifieds are made by people, determined by the culture or subculture to which they belong. They are part of the linguistic or semiotic system that members of that culture use to communicate with each other.

So, then, the area of reality or experience to which any one signified refers, that is the signification of the sign, is determined not by the nature of that reality/experience, but by the boundaries of the related signifieds in the system. Meaning is therefore better defined by the relationships of one sign to another than by the relationship of that sign to an external reality. This relationship of the sign to others in its system is what Saussure calls *value*. And for Saussure *value* is what primarily determines meaning.

45

Semiotics and meaning

Semiotics sees communication as the generation of meaning in messages – whether by the encoder or the decoder. Meaning is not an absolute, static concept to be found neatly parcelled up in the message. Meaning is an active process: semioticians use verbs like create, generate, or negotiate to refer to this process. Negotiation is perhaps the most useful in that it implies the to-and-fro, the give-and-take between person and message. Meaning is the result of the dynamic interaction between sign, interpretant, and object: it is historically located and may well change with time. It may even be useful to drop the term 'meaning' and use Peirce's far more active term 'semiosis' – the act of signifying.

Categories of signs

Basic concepts

Peirce and Saussure both tried to explain the different ways in which signs convey meaning. Peirce produced three categories of sign, each of which showed a different relationship between the sign and its object, or that to which it refers.

In an *icon* the sign resembles its object in some way: it looks or sounds like it. In an *index* there is a direct link between a sign and its object: the two are actually connected. In a *symbol* there is no connection or resemblance between sign and object: a symbol communicates only because people agree that it shall stand for what it does. A photograph is an icon, smoke is an index of fire, and a word is a symbol.

Saussure was not concerned with indexes. Indeed, as a linguist, he was really concerned only with symbols, for words are symbols. But his followers have recognized that the physical form of the sign (which Saussure called the signifier) and its associated mental concept (the signified) can be related in an *iconic* or an *arbitrary* way. In an iconic relationship, the signifier looks or sounds like the signified; in an arbitrary relationship, the two are related only by agreement among the users. What Saussure terms *iconic* and *arbitrary relations* between signifier and signified correspond precisely to Peirce's *icons* and *symbols*.

Further implications

Though Saussure and Peirce were working in the different academic traditions of linguistics and philosophy respectively, they none the less agreed on the centrality of the sign to any understanding of semiotics. They also agreed that the first task was to categorize the variety of signs in terms of the way that, for Saussure, the signifier related to the signified, or, for Peirce, the way that the sign related to the object.

Peirce and the sign

Peirce divided signs into three types – icon, index, and symbol. Once again, these can be modelled on a triangle (figure 15). Peirce felt that this was the most useful and fundamental model of the nature of signs. He writes:

> every sign is determined by its object, either first, by partaking in the character of the object, when I call the sign an *Icon*; secondly, by being really and in its individual existence connected with the individual object, when I call the sign an *Index*; thirdly, by more or less approximate certainty that it will be interpreted as denoting the object in consequence of a habit . . . when I call the sign a *Symbol*. (In Zeman, 1977)

An *icon* bears a resemblance to its object. This is often most apparent in visual signs: a photograph of my aunt is an icon; a map is an icon; the common visual signs denoting ladies' and gentlemen's lavatories are icons. But it may be verbal: onomatopoeia is an attempt to make language iconic. Tennyson's line 'The hum of bees in immemorial elms' makes the sound of the words resemble the sound of the bees. It is iconic. Beethoven's 'Pastoral' Symphony contains musical icons of natural sounds. We might think that some perfumes are artificial icons of animal smells indicating sexual arousal. Peirce's model of sign-object-interpretant is an icon in that it attempts to reproduce in concrete form the abstract structure of the relationship between its elements.

An *index* is equally simple to explain. It is a sign with a direct existential connection with its object. Smoke is an index of fire; a sneeze

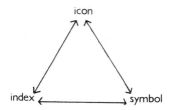

Figure 15   *Peirce's categories of sign-types*

is an index of a head cold. If I arrange to meet you and tell you that you will recognize me because I am bearded and will wear a yellow rose in my buttonhole, then my beard and yellow rose are indexes of me.

A *symbol* is a sign whose connection with its object is a matter of convention, agreement, or rule. Words are, in general, symbols. The red cross is a symbol. Numbers are symbols – there is no reason why the shape 2 should refer to a pair of objects: it is only by convention or rule in our culture that it does. The Roman number II is, of course, iconic.

These categories are not separate and distinct. One sign may be composed of various types. Take the road sign in figure 16, for example. The red triangle is a symbol – by the rule of the Highway Code it means 'warning'. The cross in the middle is a mixture of icon and symbol: it is iconic in that its form is determined partly by the shape of its object, but it is symbolic in that we need to know the rules in order to understand it as 'crossroads' and not as 'church' or 'hospital'. And the sign is, in real life, an index in that it indicates that we are about to reach a crossroads. When printed in the Highway Code, or in this book, it is not indexical in that it is not physically or spatially connected with its object.

Figure 16   *Icon-index-symbol*

Analysis

We might test the explanatory power of Peirce's sign categories by analysing the cartoons in plates 2 and 3. Cartoons are examples of messages which attempt to convey a wealth of information by simple, direct means – they use simple signifiers for complex signifieds.

Plate 2 uses the traditional cartoon convention of two men in conversation to convey a message about the Irish Troubles, industrial unrest in the Midlands, law and order, and the attitudes of the Liberal government of the day.

Plate 2   ASQUITH (to his sturdy henchman): '*No – don't worry too much about these Ulster Orangemen, but, of course, keep your eye on the Black Country. We have determined there shall be no bloodshed and violence tolerated in this country save that which is offered in the name of the Christian religion!*' Will Dyson, the *Daily Herald*, 19 June 1913

The figure on the right is Asquith, the Prime Minister. We recognize him by the way his face is drawn: it is *iconic*, which means that the form it takes is determined by the appearance of the *object* (Asquith himself). The hands in the pockets, however, are a different sort of sign. They, together with the upright posture with the weight back on the heels, may be taken to indicate nonchalance. The physical posture is an *index* of emotional attitude, in the way that smoke is an index of fire, or spots of measles. The confident hemisphere of his belly is also an index, though with a slight difference. It is an index that is approaching a metonym (see below, p. 95). A photograph of a starving baby can be an index of a

49

Third World famine, and in the same way a fat belly can be an index of prosperity and consumption (if the striking producers in the Black Country had been portrayed they would presumably have been thin and hungry). But Asquith was, himself, portly. So the belly has an iconic dimension as well. I think, too, that the receding chin is an iconic index of the same sort, indicating a moral weakness or decadence. This is my interpretant of the sign, but I feel less confident that you will share it with me than I am of my interpretant of the belly.

Dyson, the cartoonist, is exploiting an important property of icons and indexes. Because these types of sign are both connected to their objects directly, though differently, they appear to bring reality with them. They seem to say 'The object really *is* like this; your interpretant is formed by your experience of the object rather than by my sign. My sign is merely reminding you of, or is bringing you a reflection of, the object itself.' They imply that Asquith really is nonchalant, complacent, prosperous, in a more imperative way than a *symbolic* description would, such as a verbal one. Our study of news photographs in chapter 6 will develop this notion further.

Martin Walker (1978), from whom the cartoons in this chapter are taken, comments on the 'dumb stupidity and awesome backside of the policeman'. You might like to consider the way that iconic and indexical relations between the sign and the object combine with the reader's social experience of the police to produce the interpretant.

Gould's cartoon (plate 3) will also repay close analysis. Kaiser Bill is shown as a burglar stealing the family silver (Serbia and Belgium). At the window, about to catch him, is a policeman whose silhouetted mutton-chop whiskers identify him as John Bull. Britain, the policeman, is going to keep Europe safe from thieving Germany.

The silver is clearly a symbol of Serbia and Belgium. But there is no pre-existing agreement of this relationship between sign and object. So Gould has to use other *symbols*, the words SERBIA and BELGIUM, to create it. These words, of course, only communicate because their users agree that they do refer to specific countries in Europe. The mutton-chops, however, are an *index* of John Bull, and John Bull is a *symbol* of Britain (in this case, of course, the agreement does exist – we all agree that John Bull stands for Britain).

This cartoon is a complex combination of icons, indexes, and symbols that will repay much closer analysis than I have given it here. You should also return to it after reading chapter 6, when you will be able to compare Peirce's sign categories with Jakobson's theory of metaphor and metonymy.

Plate 3 *'Kaiser Bill'*. Francis Gould, the *Westminster Gazette*, August 1914

Saussure and the sign

Saussure's analysis of the sign relegates 'signification', the relationship of the signified to reality or of Peirce's sign to object, to second place. He is concerned primarily with the relationship of signifier to signified and with one sign to others. Saussure's term 'signified' has similarities with Peirce's 'interpretant', but Saussure never uses the term 'effect' to relate signifier to signified: he does not extend his interest into the realm of the user.

Saussure's interest in the relationship of signifier with signified has developed into a major concern within the European tradition of semiotics. Saussure himself concentrated on articulating a linguistic theory and made merely a passing mention of a possible area of study that he called semiology:

> We can therefore imagine *a science which would study the life of signs within society* . . . . We call it *semiology*, from the Greek *semeion* ('sign'). It would teach us what signs consist of, what laws govern them. Since it does not yet exist we cannot say what it will be: but it has a right to

existence; its place is assured in advance. Linguistics is only a part of this general science; and the laws which semiology discovers will be applicable to linguistics, which will thus find itself attached to a well-defined domain of human phenomena. (*Course*, 16; *Cours*, 33)

It has been left to his followers to work out more fully this science of signs. (Incidentally, they have worked mainly in France and tend to use the term *semiology*.)

Motivation of the sign

Two of Saussure's followers who have developed his ideas have been Pierre Guiraud (1975) and Roland Barthes (1968, 1973). To follow their analysis we shall need to learn a new set of terms. (One of the hardest aspects of any developing area of study is the amount of jargon it creates. New writers tend to coin new words, and it is only when a science becomes well established that its terminology settles down and becomes fairly widely agreed. In our case authorities cannot even agree on the name of the science itself.) The main terms used in studying the relationship between the signifier and the signified are *arbitrary*, *iconic*, *motivation*, and *constraint*, and they are all closely interconnected.

The arbitrary nature of the sign was for Saussure the heart of human language. By this he meant that there was no necessary relationship between signifier and signified: the relationship was determined by convention, rule, or agreement among the users. In other words, the signs that he called *arbitrary* correspond exactly to those that Peirce called *symbols*. Like Peirce, Saussure thought that this was the most important and highly developed category.

The term *iconic* is already familiar. Saussureans use it in the Peircean sense: that is, an iconic sign is one where the form of the signifier is determined to some extent by the signified.

The terms *motivation* and *constraint* are used to describe the extent to which the signified determines the signifier: they are almost interchangeable. A highly motivated sign is a very iconic one: a photograph is more highly motivated than a road sign. An arbitrary sign is unmotivated. Or we can use the term *constraint* to refer to the influence which the signified exerts on the signifier. The more motivated the sign is, the more its signifier is constrained by the signified.

A photograph of a man is highly motivated, for what the photograph (the signifier) looks like is determined mainly by what the man himself looks like. (The photographer's influence – framing, focus, lighting, camera angle, etc. – produces an arbitrary element in the final sign.) A painted portrait is, or can be, less iconic or more arbitrary than a photograph – it is less motivated. A cartoon (for example, that of Asquith, plate 2) is still less motivated: the cartoonist has more freedom to make the subject appear the way he wants him to; he is less constrained. If we are looking for less motivated, more arbitrary signs for 'man' that still have an iconic element, we might turn to a child's matchstick drawing, or the symbol on gentlemen's lavatories. An unmotivated, arbitrary sign is the word MAN itself, or the symbol ♂. Plate 4 illustrates this point with a collage of signs of varying degrees of motivation. The less motivated the sign is, the more important it is for us to have learnt the conventions agreed amongst the users: without them the sign remains meaningless, or liable to wildly *aberrant decoding* (see below, p. 78).

Convention

Convention, or habit in Peirce's terms, plays an important variety of roles in communication and signification. At its most formal level it can describe the rules by which arbitrary signs work. There is a formal convention that the sign CAT refers to a four-legged feline animal and not an article of clothing. There is a formal convention that fixes the meaning of three signs in this order with this grammatical form: CATS HUNT RATS: we agree that the first word chases the third. It is also conventional that a final -s means plurality.

But there are also less formal, less explicitly expressed, conventions. We have learnt by experience that slow motion on television 'means' one of two things: either analysis of skill or error (particularly in sports programmes), or appreciation of beauty. Sometimes, as in women's gymnastics, it means both. Our experience of similar signs, that is our experience of the convention, enables us to respond appropriately – we know that it does not mean that people have suddenly started running slow laps; and our experience of the content tells us whether we are meant to appreciate the beauty or evaluate the skill of the movement.

Sometimes it is difficult to determine the relative parts played by convention and iconicity in a sign – that is, how highly motivated or constrained a sign actually is. A television camera zooming into close-up on someone's face conventionally means that that person is experiencing a strong emotion of some sort. We know, by convention, that it does not mean that we have suddenly pushed our face to within inches of his or hers. But that zoom also has an iconic element in that it represents, or

Plate 4 *Signs of women*

54

reproduces, the focusing of our interest upon a person at such a moment.

Convention is necessary to the understanding of any sign, however iconic or indexical it is. We need to learn how to understand a photograph or even a life-size waxwork. Convention is the social dimension of signs (see also p. 77): it is the agreement amongst the users about the appropriate uses of and responses to a sign. Signs with no conventional dimension are purely private and thus do not communicate. So it may be of more help to consider the distinction between arbitrary and iconic signs or between symbols and icons/indexes as a scale, not as separate categories. At one end of the scale we have the purely arbitrary sign, the symbol. At the other end we have the notional pure icon, which cannot, of course, exist in practice. We can visualize the scale as in figure 17.

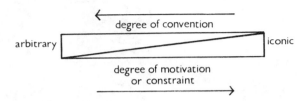

Figure 17 *Scale of motivation*

At the left-hand end of the scale are the signs that are 100 per cent arbitrary, conventional, unmotivated, unconstrained. In the middle are mixed signs, placed according to their degree of motivation. Thus the cross indicating a crossroads on a road sign would be further to the left than a map of a particular crossroads. The former we might estimate as 60 per cent arbitrary, 40 per cent iconic, whereas the latter may be 30/70 per cent. And we ought to chop off the last half-an-inch on the right, unless the development of holograms makes the purely iconic sign a possibility.

The organization of signs

Basic concepts

Saussure defined two ways in which signs are organized into codes. The first is by *paradigms*. A paradigm is a set of signs from which the one to be used is chosen. The set of shapes for road signs – square, round, or triangular – forms a paradigm; so does the set of symbols that can go within them. Saussure's second way is the *syntagmatic*. A syntagm is the message into which the chosen signs are combined. A road sign is a syntagm, a combination of the chosen shape with the chosen symbol. In language, we can say that the vocabulary is the paradigm, and a sentence is a syntagm. So all messages involve *selection* (from a paradigm) and *combination* (into a syntagm).

Further implications

We must remember that Saussure insisted that a sign's meaning was determined mainly by its relationship to other signs. It is here that his linguistic interest shows most strongly, and it is in this that he differs most radically from Peirce. The two main types of relationship which a sign can form with others are described by the terms *paradigm* and *syntagm*.

Paradigms

Let us take paradigms first. A paradigm is a set from which a choice is made and only one unit from that set may be chosen. A simple example is the letters of the alphabet. These form the paradigm for written language and illustrate the two basic characteristics of a paradigm:

(i) All the units in a paradigm must have something in common: they must share characteristics that determine their membership of that paradigm. We must know that M is a letter and thus a member of the alphabetic paradigm, and we must recognize equally that 5 is not, and neither is ÷.

(ii) Each unit must be clearly distinguished from all the others in the paradigm. We must be able to tell the difference between signs in a paradigm in terms of both their signifiers and their signifieds. The means by which we distinguish one signifier from another are called the *distinctive features* of a sign: this is a concept of considerable analytical importance to which we will return later. In our current example we need to say only that bad handwriting is handwriting that blurs the distinctive features of the letters.

Every time we communicate we must select from a paradigm. Words are a paradigm – the vocabulary of English is a paradigm. Words are also categorized into other, more specific paradigms: grammatical paradigms, such as nouns or verbs; paradigms of use – baby language, legal language, lovers' talk, masculine swearing; or paradigms of sound – words that rhyme, day, may, say, etc. At a more detailed level still, the three Saussurian terms for analysing the sign form a paradigm and are frequently written Sn, Sr, Sd. Here the S indicates by convention the paradigm and the -n, -r, -d, are the distinctive features that identify the units within it.

Other examples of paradigms are: way of changing shot in television – cut, fade, dissolve, wipe, etc.; headgear – trilby, cap, beret, stetson, etc.; the style of chairs with which we furnish our living room; the type of car we drive; the colour we paint our front door. All these involve paradigmatic choices, and the meaning of the unit we choose is determined largely by the meanings of the units we did not. We can sum up by saying 'where there is choice there is meaning, and the meaning of what was chosen is determined by the meaning of what was not'.

Syntagms

Once a unit has been chosen from a paradigm it is normally combined with other units. This combination is called a *syntagm*. Thus a written word is a visual syntagm composed of a sequence of paradigmatic choices from the letters of the alphabet. A sentence is a syntagm of words. Our clothes are a syntagm of choices from the paradigms of hats, ties, shirts, jackets, trousers, socks, etc. The way we furnish a room is a syntagm of choices from the paradigms of chairs, tables, settees, carpets, wallpapers, etc. An architect designing a house makes a syntagm of the styles of doors, windows, etc., and their positions. A menu is a good example of a complete *system*. The choices for each course (the paradigms) are given in full: each diner combines them into a meal: the order given to the waiter is a syntagm.

The important aspect of syntagms is the rules or conventions by which the combination of units is made. In language we call this grammar or syntax; in music we call it melody (harmony is a matter of paradigmatic choice); in clothes we call it good taste, or fashion sense, though there are more formal rules as well. For instance, a black bow-tie with a black jacket and white collar means a dinner guest, but the same bow-tie with a tailed coat and a white wing collar would mean a waiter. In a syntagm, then, the chosen sign can be affected by its relationship with others; its meaning is determined partly by its relationship with others in the syntagm.

For Saussure, and the structural linguists who followed him, the key to understanding signs was to understand their structural relationship with others. There are two types of structural relationship – paradigmatic, that of choice; or syntagmatic, that of combination.

Traffic lights

Traffic lights are a simple communication system that we can use to illustrate many of the analytical concepts introduced in this chapter. Figure 18 shows how Edmund Leach (1974) models the structural relationships of traffic lights. If we analyse the signifying in full we start by identifying the paradigm – that is, of traffic lights. A red light here means STOP and not BROTHEL or RECORDING IN PROGRESS. It is arbitrary, or a symbol, but not entirely so. Red is so widespread a sign for danger that we are justified in looking for some iconic element in it. It may be because it is the colour of blood, or because in moments of extreme rage or fear, the dilation of the blood vessels in the eye literally makes us 'see red'. So red is a crisis colour. If red, by a mixture of convention and motivation, means 'stop', the rest follows logically. Green is the opposite of red on the colour spectrum, as GO is the opposite of STOP. Colour is the distinctive feature, and green is as distinctive from red as is possible. If we need a third unit in the system, we ought to go for yellow or blue, as these colours are midway between red and green in the spectrum. Blue is reserved for emergency services, so the choice is naturally yellow, or amber to give it a stronger form. Then we introduce a simple syntax: amber combined with red is a syntagm meaning that the change is in the direction of GO; amber on its own means that the change is in the direction of STOP. Other rules are that red can never be combined with green, and that red and green can never follow each other directly.

So there is a lot of redundancy built into the system. A red light is all that is strictly needed: 'on' for STOP, 'off' for GO. But even temporary traffic lights add redundancy by including a green. This prevents the possible error of decoding 'off' as 'the lights have broken down'. The full

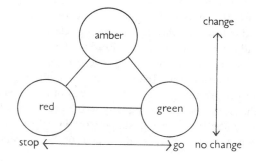

Figure 18   *Traffic lights*

system, of course, has high redundancy because it is vital to minimize errors of decoding and there may be a lot of 'noise' (the sun in the eyes, other traffic to concentrate on).

Suggestions for further work

1. Apply Peirce's model to different types of sign: for example, a facial expression indicating boredom; a road sign for HALT, MAJOR ROAD AHEAD; words like *gay*, *queer*, or *homosexual*; an abstract painting; somebody's style of dress; $3 + 8 = 11$. What does this tell you about the way that the interpretant is created? Does the sign or our experience of the object play the larger part in the formation of our interpretant? How does their relative importance vary? How far can my interpretant differ from yours, and how far must they be similar? Does the degree of motivation play a major part in determining the relationship and variation of meaning that you were discussing? (See Guiraud, 1975, pp. 25–7.) Discuss fully this notion of the motivation of the sign. Find examples to illustrate the range.

2. Analyse plates 5 and 6. Use Peirce's and Saussure's concepts and compare their comparative usefulness. How necessary do you think Walker's comments are? Do they help bridge the cultural gap caused by the passage of time? Are they equally helpful for each cartoon?

3. Barthes (1973), pp. 112–13 uses roses as an example of a sign: a rose is a physical object, but if I present it to my lady-love I invest it with a signified – a type of romantic passion. It has now become a signifier, and the presented rose has become a sign. Compare this with the example OX in this chapter (p. 44). How far do these examples help to explain Saussure's terms signifier, signified, and sign? Do they explain them differently than the example of a word would? If so, why?

4. Discuss fully the implications of the theory that signifieds are arbitrary and culture-specific. Does it help to clarify the idea that we see the world through our language? Read Culler (1976), pp. 18–29.

5. News photographs and magazine advertisements are frequently indexical and always iconic. Take an example of either (or both) and analyse it in Peirce's terms to test the accuracy of this assertion. (You may find that it does not apply equally well to each.) Study the way that words (symbols) are used to support the visual signs. Return to this question after you have read chapter 6. See Hawkes (1977), pp. 123–30.

6. Turn to plate 4. Arrange the signs in it in order of their degree of

Plate 5 *'BRAVO BELGIUM!'* F. H. Townsend, *Punch*, 12 August 1914. Walker (1978) comments: 'The villainous old bully with his sausages and his big stick leads us to hate the Germans, and the plucky, clean-cut, defiant youngster brings out all our sympathy for the Belgian allies. This cartoon idea has been used and borrowed and circulated endlessly. In July 1933, when Hitler was threatening to occupy Austria, *Punch* copied the Townsend idea, with a gallant little Austria before the same farm gate, and a bullying Hitler waving the same old stick. But they forgot the sausages.'

motivation and place them upon the scale on p. 56. Give reasons for your decisions. In your discussion you should use terms like convention, agreement, arbitrary, iconic, motivation, constraint. You may also find the terms signifier, signified, symbol, index, interpretant, and object necessary. Using the jargon helps you to familiarize yourself with it and to see the point of it. The plate is part of the paradigm 'signs of women': how much does each sign in

Plate 6 *'STILL HOPE'*. Ilingworth, *Punch*, 21 September 1938. Walker (1978) comments: 'It is almost ungallant to *Punch* and to Chamberlain to reproduce this tribute to Appeasement. Europe had been on the brink of war: gas masks had been issued in London, and trenches dug in Hyde Park. And then came the Munich settlement and the collective sigh of relief. It is hindsight, and perhaps the prescience of prophets such as Low, which lead us to mock the Appeasers today. But the feeling that almost anything was better than war (particularly a war as long and costly as 1914–18) and that Germany did have legitimate complaints against the Peace of Versailles, was a testimony to fairness in British public life. It is, however, worth recalling that Chamberlain had taken out insurance in February 1937, when he announced a £1500 million re-armament programme. By the outbreak of war, Britain was producing each month as many tanks and more war planes as Hitler's Germany.'

it depend for its meaning upon the reader's familiarity with the rest of the paradigm? Why is the 100 per cent icon impossible?

7. Analyse how we decode bad handwriting. You should use terms like predictability (chapter 1), perception (Gerbner's model, chapter 2), distinctive features, and signifier/signified. How far does this relate to reading a blurred photograph, or an indistinct photograph of the moon, or talking to someone in a noisy disco?

8. Take a sentence and a photograph. Both are syntagms composed of units chosen from paradigms. How far does identifying the paradigm and the syntagm help towards an understanding of the meaning of each? (See Fiske and Hartley, 1978, pp. 50–8.)

You may find the following useful background reading: Culler (1976), pp. 18–52; Cherry (1957), pp. 112–17, 221–3, 265–9; Guiraud (1975), pp. 1–4, 22–9.

4 CODES

Codes

Basic concepts

What we have been studying, in our analysis of traffic lights, is a code. Codes are, in fact, the systems into which signs are organized. These systems are governed by rules which are consented to by all members of the community using that code. This means that the study of codes frequently emphasizes the *social* dimension of communication.

Almost any aspect of our social life which is conventional, or governed by rules consented to by members of the society, can therefore be called 'coded'. We need to distinguish between *codes of behaviour*, such as the legal code, the code of manners, or the two codes of rugby, and *signifying codes*. Signifying codes are systems of signs. Having made the distinction, we must recognize that the two categories of code are interconnected. The Highway Code is both a behavioural and a signifying system. Bernstein's work links the language people use with their social life. No signifying code can be properly divorced from the social practices of its users.

In this book, though, we concentrate on the second category of code. Indeed, I use the word code to mean signifying system. All codes of this type have a number of basic features.

1. They have a number of units (or sometimes one unit) from which a selection is made. This is the paradigmatic dimension. These units (on all except the simplest on–off single-unit codes) may be combined by rules or conventions. This is the syntagmatic dimension.

2. All codes convey meaning: their units are signs which refer, by various means, to something other than themselves.
3. All codes depend upon an agreement amongst their users and upon a shared cultural background. Codes and culture interrelate dynamically.
4. All codes perform an identifiable social or communicative function.
5. All codes are transmittable by their appropriate media and/or channels of communication.

In this chapter we shall cover all of these features, but shall concentrate mainly on features 3 and 4. Feature 2 has been dealt with at some length in chapter 3, and feature 5 in chapter 1. First, though, it will be helpful to recapitulate some of the work we have already covered on the nature of the units that constitute a code and to introduce two new terms: *analogue* and *digital*.

Analogue and digital codes

Basic concepts

We have seen (p. 57) that paradigms are composed of units with an overall similarity, but with distinctive features that distinguish them one from another. There are two types of paradigm which give their names to two types of code: analogue and digital. A digital code is one whose units (both signifiers and signifieds) are clearly separated; an analogue code is one that works on a continuous scale. A digital watch separates one minute from the next: it is either five minutes past or six minutes past. An analogue watch has a continuous scale and it is only by putting marks on the dial that we can read it 'digitally'.

Digital codes are easier to understand simply because their units are clearly distinguished. Arbitrary codes are digital, and this makes them easy to write down or notate. Music is potentially an analogue code, though our system of notation has given it distinctive features (the notes and scales) and thus imposed upon it the characteristics of a digital code. Dance, though, is analogic. It works through gestures, posture, distance – all analogue codes and thus difficult to notate. Nature is generally composed of analogues: in trying to understand or categorize nature, we impose digital differences upon it: for example, the 'seven ages of man'; or intimate, personal, semi-public and public distances between people.

Further implications

This search for significant differences or distinctive features is crucial to the textual side of meaning. In arbitrary or symbolic codes it is a straightforward process, for if the units of a paradigm are stated and agreed, the differences between them must be identified.

Codes composed of iconic signs, however, pose problems. We will see how the commutation test (p. 109), or Baggaley and Duck's work with the semantic differential (p. 145), have attempted to identify what features of an iconic message are significant. Fiske and Hartley (1978) have discussed in some detail the problems and importance of identifying this 'smallest signifying unit' in a code. Our semiotic analysis of a news photograph (p. 104) will show that these distinctive features may be significant only in the second order of signification. The codes of photography pose particular problems, because photography appears to follow nature in being composed of analogical scales. The search for meaning, however, involves the identification of significant differences and thus the imposition of digital features upon an analogical reality. Putting sixty marks around the perimeter of a clockface is a metaphor of how we impose meaning upon reality.

So the perception of reality is itself an encoding process. Perception involves making sense of the data before us: it involves identifying significant differences and thus identifying units – what we are perceiving. It then involves the perception of the relationship between these units, so that we can see them as a whole. In other words, it involves creating paradigms and syntagms. Our perception and understanding of reality is as specific to our culture as our language is. It is in this sense that we talk of reality as a social construct.

Presentational codes

But codes are not just systems for organizing and understanding data: they perform communicative and social functions. One way to categorize these functions is to distinguish between representational and presentational codes.

Representational codes are used to produce *texts*, that is messages with an independent existence. A text stands for something apart from itself and its encoder. A text is composed of iconic or symbolic signs. Most of this book and much of the rest of this chapter is concerned with understanding texts composed of representational codes. Presentational codes are indexical: they cannot stand for something apart from themselves and their encoder. They indicate aspects of the communicator and of her or his present social situation.

Non-verbal communication

Basic concepts

Non-verbal communication (or NVC) is carried on through presentational codes such as gestures, eye movements, or qualities of voice. These codes can give messages only about the here and now. My tone of voice can indicate my present attitude to my subject and listener: it cannot send a message about my feelings last week. Presentational codes, then, are limited to face-to-face communication or communication when the communicator is present. They have two functions.

The first, as we have seen, is to convey indexical information. This is information about the speaker and his or her situation through which the listener learns about her or his identity, emotions, attitudes, social position, and so on. The second function is interaction management. The codes are used to manage the sort of relationship the encoder wants with the other. By using certain gestures, posture, and tone of voice, I can attempt to dominate my fellows, be conciliatory towards them or shut myself off from them. I can use codes to indicate that I have finished speaking and it is someone else's turn, or to indicate my desire to terminate the meeting. These codes are still, in a sense, indexical, but they are used to convey information about the relationship rather than about the speaker.

These two functions of presentational codes can also be performed by the representational in so far as presentational codes can be present in representational messages. A written text can have a 'tone of voice'; a photograph can convey depression or joy. But social psychologists recognize a third function of codes which can be performed only by the representational. This is the cognitive or ideational. This is the function of conveying information or ideas about things absent, and it involves the creation of a message or a text that is independent of the communicator and situation. Verbal language or photography are examples of representational codes. Jakobson's model (see p. 35) can clarify the difference between the two types of code. Representational codes are the only ones that can perform the referential function. Presentational codes are most efficient in the conative and emotive functions. Both types of code work on the aesthetic and the phatic, though the metalinguistic is confined largely to the representational.

Further implications

The human body is the main transmitter of presentational codes. Argyle (1972) lists ten such codes and suggests the sort of meanings they can convey.

1. *Bodily contact* Whom we touch and where and when we touch them can convey important messages about relationships. Interestingly, this code and the next (proximity) are ones that appear to vary most between people of different cultures. The British touch each other less frequently than members of almost any other culture.

2. *Proximity (or proxemics)* How closely we approach someone can give a message about our relationship. There appear to be 'distinctive features' that differentiate significantly different distances. Within three feet is intimate; up to about eight feet is personal; over eight feet is semi-public; and so on. The actual distances may vary from culture to culture: the personal, but not intimate, distance of Arabs can be as little as eighteen inches – which can be very embarrassing for a British listener. Middle-class distances tend to be slightly larger than the corresponding working-class ones.

3. *Orientation* How we angle ourselves to others is another way of sending messages about relationships. Facing someone can indicate either intimacy or aggression; being at 90° to another indicates a co-operative stance; and so on.

4. *Appearance* Argyle divides this into two: those aspects under voluntary control – hair, clothes, skin, bodily paint and adornment – and those less controllable – height, weight, etc. Hair is, in all cultures, highly significant as it is the most 'flexible' part of our bodies: we can most easily alter its appearance. Appearance is used to send messages about personality, social status, and, particularly, conformity. Teenagers frequently indicate their dissatisfaction with adult values by hair and dress: and then complain when such messages of hostility provoke negative reactions from adults!

5. *Head nods* These are involved mainly in interaction management, particularly in turn-taking in speech. One nod may give the other permission to carry on speaking; rapid nods may indicate a wish to speak.

6. *Facial expression* This may be broken down into the sub-codes of eyebrow position, eye shape, mouth shape, and nostril size. These, in various combinations, determine the expression of the face, and it is possible to write a 'grammar' of their combinations and meanings. Interestingly, facial expression shows less cross-cultural variation than most other presentational codes.

7. *Gestures (or kinesics)* The hand and arm are the main transmitters of gesture, but gestures of feet and head are also important. They are closely co-ordinated with speech and supplement verbal communication. They may indicate either general emotional arousal or specific emotional states. The intermittent, emphatic up-and-down gesture often indicates an attempt to dominate, whereas more fluid, continuous, circular gestures indicate a desire to explain or to win sympathy. Besides these indexical gestures, there is a group of symbolic ones. These are frequently insulting or scatological and are specific to a culture or subculture: the V sign is an example. We should also mention the iconic type of gesture such as beckoning, or using the hands to describe a shape or direction.

8. *Posture* Our ways of sitting, standing, and lying can communicate a limited but interesting range of meanings. These are frequently concerned with interpersonal attitudes: friendliness, hostility, superiority or inferiority can all be indicated by posture. Posture can also indicate emotional state, particularly the degree of tension or relaxation. Interestingly, and perhaps surprisingly, posture is less well controlled than facial expression: anxiety that does not show on the face may well be given away by posture.

9. *Eye movement and eye contact* When, how often, and for how long we meet other people's eyes is a way of sending very important messages about relationships, particularly how dominant or affiliative we wish the relationship to be. Staring someone out is a simple challenge of dominance; making eyes at someone indicates a desire for affiliation. Making eye contact at the beginning of or early in a verbal statement indicates a desire to dominate the listener, to make him or her pay attention; eye contact towards the end of or after a verbal statement indicates a more affiliative relationship, a desire for feedback, to see how the listener is reacting.

10. *Non-verbal aspects of speech* These are divided into two categories:
    (a) The prosodic codes which affect the meaning of the words used.

Pitch and stress are the main codes here. 'The shops are open on Sunday' can be made into a statement, a question, or an expression of disbelief by the pitch of the voice.

(b) The paralinguistic codes which communicate information about the speaker. Tone, volume, accent, speech errors, and speed indicate the speaker's emotional state, personality, class, social status, way of viewing the listener, and so on.

These presentational codes are classified by their medium. They are all relatively simple, in that they have comparatively few units to choose from in the paradigmatic dimension, and very simple rules of combination in the syntagmatic. They are, in fact, broadly similar to what Bernstein calls 'restricted' codes.

Elaborated and restricted codes

Basic concepts

This famous classification of code is the work of Basil Bernstein (for example 1964, 1973). He is a socio-linguist and has concentrated his work on the language of children. So these terms apply originally to different uses of verbal language, though we may now legitimately extend them to cover other types of code. Bernstein's work has been highly controversial because he links the types of language used with the social class of the user and relates this to the educational system. He has taken linguistics into politics.

He found that there were fundamental differences in the speech of working-class and middle-class children, and he summarized these differences by claiming that working-class children tended to use a restricted code and middle-class children an elaborated code. Later, he stressed what some of his critics have ignored, and this is that social class is not of itself the determining factor. What actually determines the code used is the type of social relations that exist. Thus a tight, closed, traditional community tends to use restricted codes. The working class is one example of such a community, but so too are middle-class institutions such as the officers' mess, the legal profession, or a boys' public school: each of these communities uses its own type of restricted code.

The more fluid, changing, mobile, impersonal type of social relations typical of the modern middle class tends to produce an elaborated linguistic code. Bernstein's final point is that the working classes are confined to a restricted code, whereas the middle classes can move from a restricted to an elaborated code at will.

Further implications

But what are the characteristics of these two types of code?

1. The restricted code is *simpler*, less complex than the elaborated. It has a smaller vocabulary and simpler syntax.
2. The restricted code tends to be oral and thus is closer to the presentational, indexical codes of non-verbal communication. The elaborated code can be written or spoken and thus is better for representational, symbolic messages.
3. The restricted code tends to be redundant. Its messages are highly predictable and are likely to perform phatic rather than referential functions. The elaborated code is more entropic; it is harder to predict the verbal options open to the speaker. It is more capable of the referential function.
4. The restricted code is orientated towards social relations; the elaborated facilitates the expression of the individual's discrete intent. This means that the restricted code is indexical of the speaker's status within the group. It reinforces social relations and expresses the similarities between speaker and group, restricting the signalling of individual differences. The elaborated code, on the other hand, is geared towards the individual as a person, rather than a status role within a group; it copes with the speaker's expectation of psychological difference between him- or herself and the listener(s) and therefore facilitates the expression of individuality – where he or she differs from the listener(s). The restricted code facilitates the expression of commonality, of group membership – what the speaker shares with the listener(s).

    The restricted code, then, depends on a background of common assumptions, shared interests, shared experience, identifications, and expectations. It depends on a local cultural identity which reduces the need for speakers to verbalize their individual experience.

    The elaborated code, then, is necessary when the speaker wishes to verbalize precise meanings that are personally unique, but which he or she wishes to make available to the listener. Communication depends not on a local commonality, but on the shared arbitrary code of language which enables the elaboration of intended meaning.

5. Restricted codes rely on interaction with non-verbal codes. Indeed,

Bernstein suggests that individual differences are expressed only through non-verbal codes: speech is used to express commonality. Elaborated codes play down NVC, which is why the written language is almost invariably elaborated.

6. Restricted codes express the concrete, the specific, the here and now; elaborated express abstractions, generalities, the absent.

7 Restricted codes depend on cultural experience; elaborated on formal education and training — they need to be learnt.

To help recognize the restricted code of speech, Bernstein suggests that we imagine ourselves eavesdropping on a group of friends on a street corner. We would note the following:

1. We would be aware of our own exclusion from the group or community.

2. We would note that the speech was relatively impersonal, less individualistic: it would contain more 'you' and 'they', less 'I'; it would contain more phrases like 'isn't it', 'you see', 'you know', phrases which express the commonality of the speaker, and fewer expressions of individualism.

3. We would note the vitality, the liveliness of the speech. What matters is *how* something is said, not *what* is said. Much of the real meaning, and all the individuality, of the speaker would be conveyed through the non-verbal codes.

4. We would note that the speech flow was dislocated, disjunctive. The organization of ideas is based on association, not on logic or syntactic sequence.

5. We would note that the content was concrete, narrative, descriptive, not analytical or abstract.

6. We would note a restricted vocabulary and syntax.

Bernstein gives an example of lower-working-class speech which illustrates these points.

It's all according like well these youths and that if they get with gangs and that they most they most have a bit of a lark around and say it goes wrong and that and they probably knock some off I think they do it just to be a bit big you know getting publicity here and there.

Codes and value judgements

Our society clearly values the elaborated codes. English-teaching in school concentrates on and rewards the elaborated, written language. We value the highbrow forms of art which all use elaborated codes. Ballet is an elaborated dance form with a complex structure which requires formal education and training; disco dance is restricted and requires social or community experience rather than formal training. Folk stories or scatological jokes are restricted, the highbrow novel elaborated. And so we could continue. The culturally valued art forms are almost all elaborated.

Even the words that Bernstein has chosen – elaborated and restricted – have positive and negative social values. But if we are to make the most of Bernstein's work, we must discard these value judgements. Elaborated codes are not *better* than restricted codes, they are *different* and perform different functions. We are all of us individuals, we all community or group members. We need restricted and elaborated codes equally. *Coronation Street*, and popular art of this sort, actually does more to keep our scattered diverse society together by providing a shared experience than does a highbrow, culturally valued play by Samuel Beckett. The terms 'restricted' and 'elaborated' must be seen as descriptive and analytical: allowing value judgements to become attached to them will merely obscure the issue.

Broadcast and narrowcast codes

Basic concepts

Elaborated and restricted codes are defined by the nature of the code itself and by the type of social relationship it serves. Broadcast and narrowcast codes, on the other hand, are defined by the nature of the audience. A broadcast code is one that is shared by members of a mass audience: it has to cater for a degree of heterogeneity. A narrowcast code, on the other hand, is one aimed at a specific audience, often one defined by the codes that it uses. We can say that an operatic aria is using a narrowcast code: it appeals to opera-lovers; whereas a pop song is designed to appeal to a mass, non-defined audience, and is therefore using a broadcast code. This immediately highlights similarities between, on the one hand, narrowcast and elaborated codes and, on the other, broadcast and restricted.

Broadcast codes: further implications

Broadcast codes share many characteristics with restricted. They are simple; they have an immediate appeal; and they do not require an 'education' to understand them. They are community-orientated, appealing to what people have in common and tending to link them to their society. They are frequently anonymous, or at least have 'institutional' authors: Granada Television is the 'author' of *Coronation Street*. The fact that the authors are anonymous or institutional militates against the expression of the personal, individualist viewpoint. The broadcast codes are the means by which a culture communicates with itself. Stuart Hall (1973a) makes a similar point well when he talks of the television audience as being both source and receiver of the message. Seeing the audience as the source of a message may seem paradoxical and needing of further explanation.

There are three ways in which the audience can be said to originate the broadcast message. The first is in the content. If a broadcast is to receive the mass reception it needs, it must deal with matters of general concern. The 'good' mass communicator is one who is in tune with the feelings and concerns of society at large. But content is not just the subject matter of the message; it is also the way that the subject matter is handled. There are patterns of feelings, attitudes, values within a culture that are presented in its broadcast messages. These messages then re-enter the culture from which they originated, cultivating this pattern of thought and feeling. There is a constant, dynamic interaction between audience as source, broadcasting, and audience as destination. Our analysis of the front page of the *Daily Mirror* (plate 1b, p. 17) has shown how these patterns of thought and feeling have influenced the editorial construction of that message – the audience (via the editor's professional perception of it) was in a real sense the source of the message.

The second aspect of the audience as source is the way in which the audience determines the form of the message. At the simplest level this may result in the 'formula productions' by which broadcasters produce new versions of old structures. The audience has certain expectations, based on a cultural experience shared with the broadcasters, that, for instance, broadcast messages have a beginning, a middle, and an end. An event may not have finished, but a news report on it must have a conclusion: threads introduced into a naturalistic story must all be tied up and related in a most unnatural way. This same process can be traced at less obvious levels. Stuart Hall, with Connell and Curti (1976), has shown how the fact that we live in a parliamentary democracy with a 'watchdog' press determined the form of a particular *Panorama* programme. The form of the programme was conventional: representatives of the main political parties and an 'uncommitted' media chairman debated a political issue. By a careful analysis of the way in which the politicians shared the broadcast time, took turns, and by the way in which the media chairman treated them and behaved himself, the researchers demonstrated that the real meaning of the programme was not derived from the subject of the debate, but from its form: this meaning was that our system of parliamentary democracy *works*, and that the media institutions demonstrate it working. The mass audience 'knows' this well already; the 'form' of the programme proves it. This form is an encoded message: it is composed of units of television behaviour combined according to conventional syntagmatic practice. It is a broadcast code, it is a restricted code: and the cultural experience of the audience is the source of the message.

The third way in which the audience can be seen as the source is a development of this analysis. Broadcasting is an institutional activity and institutions are a product of their parent society. Britain, the United States, and Russia, for instance, are different societies and have consequently different broadcasting institutions. These institutions are staffed and run by what each society feels is an appropriate type of person; the priorities within each institution are the product of their staff and their society, and all of these add up to influence the type of broadcasting that each institution produces.

Stuart Hall argues that there is a hidden but determining relationship between the structures of thought and feeling in the audience, the encoded structure of the broadcast message, and the structures of the broadcasting institutions. All are interdependent, interdeterminate.

Fiske and Hartley (1978) have developed the concept of 'bardic television'. In this, they suggest that television performs seven functions in a modern society that the bard performed in a traditional society. These are as follows:

1. to articulate the main lines of the established cultural consensus about the nature of reality;
2. to implicate the individual members of the culture into its dominant value systems, by cultivating these systems and showing them working in practice;
3. to celebrate, explain, interpret, and justify the doings of the culture's individual representatives;
4. to assure the culture at large of its practical adequacy in the world by affirming and confirming its ideologies/mythologies in active engagement with the practical and potentially unpredictable world;
5. to expose, conversely, any practical inadequacies in the culture's sense of itself which might result from changed conditions in the world out there, or from pressure within the culture for a

reorientation in favour of a new ideological stance;

6. to convince the audience that their status and identity as individuals is guaranteed by the culture as a whole;

7. to transmit by these means a sense of cultural membership (security and involvement).

These functions are performed by all television messages: audience members negotiate their response with reference to their own particular circumstances, and by so doing situate themselves in their culture. The message is anonymous or from an institutional source: the traditional bard was a 'role' in his society, not an individual as the artist is today. Thus none of these seven functions encompasses the expression of the individual's discrete intent. They are appropriately performed by broadcast codes in a mass society and by restricted codes in a subculture or a local community. This similarity of social function between broadcast and restricted codes explains why the two share so many features.

Narrowcast codes: further implications

A corresponding set of similarities exists between narrowcast and elaborated codes. Narrowcast codes are aimed at a defined, limited audience: usually one which has decided to learn the codes involved. They need distinguishing from restricted codes (which may also be understood by a small audience only) in that they do not rely on a shared communal experience, but on a common educational or intellectual experience. The music of Stockhausen or a specialist talk on Radio 3 are examples of narrowcast codes. They are individualist, person-orientated, not communal, status-orientated. They expect differences between communicator and audience, if only that the communicator knows more, or sees and feels differently. The audience expects to be changed or enriched by the communication, whereas the audience of broadcast, restricted codes expects reassurance and confirmation.

Narrowcast codes may be élitist or, at least, socially divisive. In art they are highbrow and culturally valued; in science they produce impressive specialist jargon that the expert uses as an index of his expertise. The exclusiveness of the medical and legal professions is due in no small measure to the narrowcast codes that they use. A sociologist who uses an impressive specialist term to refer to a piece of familiar social experience is indicating her difference from the layman, her membership of a sociological élite. Communication specialists are not immune from this either. Narrowcast codes have acquired the function in our mass society of stressing the difference between 'us' (the users of the code) and 'them' (the laymen, the lowbrows). Broadcast codes stress the similarities amongst 'us' (the majority).

Codes and commonality

All codes rely on commonality, that is an agreement amongst their users on their basics — the units they contain, the rules by which these units may be selected and combined, the meanings open to the receiver, and the social or communicative function they perform. But how this agreement is reached and the form that it takes can vary considerably. We consider three significant ways of reaching agreement: by convention and use, by explicit agreement, and by clues within the text.

Convention and use

The first and most important way of reaching agreement is by convention and use. By this we mean the unwritten, unstated expectations that derive from the shared experience of members of a culture. Convention gives rise to expectations that people will dress or behave within certain limits, that television programmes or conversation will follow broadly familiar lines, that houses and their gardens will conform more or less to local or national practice. Convention relies on redundancy: it makes for easy decoding, it expresses cultural membership, it relies on similarity of experience, it is reassuring. It can also produce conformity, lack of originality, resistance to change. The agreements that are reached by convention are usually, but not always, unstated. This means that there is no formal paradigm of signifieds to parallel the paradigm of signifiers. Let us take the code of dress as an example.

Each type of clothing constitutes a paradigm — ties, shirts, jackets, trousers, socks. Dressing in the morning is encoding a message. We select a unit from each paradigm and combine it with others to make a statement. This statement uses a presentational, indexical code and conveys a meaning about (1) us as the wearer of the clothes, (2) our perception of our relationships with the people we expect to meet, and (3) our status or role within the social situations we shall come across during the day. Comparatively few clothes have defined meanings; that is, there is rarely a stated agreement amongst their users. When there is, they belong properly under our next heading, that of arbitrary codes. Examples are club ties, uniforms, or badges. These all denote signifieds in the first order of meaning: they are symbolic. The code of dress usually works, however, by indexical codes. I indicate my social position by the way I dress. My choice of tie can also connote my mood – 'I feel like wearing my blue-and-white spots today'. The eccentric dress of the artist is a way of connoting lack of respect for social convention generally. The indexical nature of clothes often makes people feel very personally about them. The young man who attends a job interview wearing jeans may explain his behaviour by saying 'They must take me as I am: I *am* a jeans-wearer.' The index has become what it indicates. The employer may well read this as indicating a resistance to the convention of the firm and thus may not offer him the job. Jeans can connote disrespect and rebelliousness.

These misunderstandings are due to the way that the employer and the interviewee have different subcultural experience of jeans. This difference of 'reading' that derives from different experience is what Eco (1965) refers to as *aberrant decoding*. When an artist produces a message for a defined audience using shared codes – when, that is, s/he produces a narrowcast message – s/he can expect that the range of meanings negotiated by audience members will be very limited. Their decoding will approximate closely to the encoding. But if that message is read by a member of a different culture who brings different codes to it, aberrant decoding will produce a different meaning. The problem occurs mainly with iconic codes – verbal languages are usually so different that *no* decoding is possible. Prehistoric cave paintings of animals have normally been read as conveying graceful, light-footed movement that seems to defy the law of gravity: but Margaret Abercrombie (1960) has argued that the paintings are, in fact, of dead animals lying on their sides. Our love of living animals and distaste for dead bodies has led us into an aberrant decoding (see plate 7). A message encoded in the codes of one culture has been decoded by the codes of another. I recently saw a recording of a Russian television news item which used British news film of a clash between police and pickets outside a factory gate. The aberrant decoding was obvious.

Because the mass media have to cater for numerous subcultures whose codes might differ significantly from those of the broadcasters, aberrant decoding becomes the rule, not the exception, with mass-media messages (Eco, 1965). When we talk about the culture of a mass society we are talking about a far more varied and loosely defined body of codes, beliefs, and practices than when we refer to the culture of, say, a tribal society. Aberrant decoding results, then, when different codes are used in the encoding and decoding of the message.

In many cases, and that of the interviewee in jeans is one, it is useful to

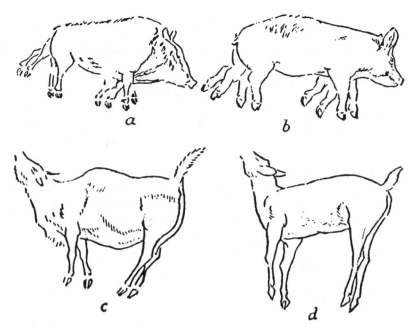

Plate 7 *Aberrant decoding. Cave paintings and dead animals.* Tracings from
the Abbé Breuil's drawings of Altamira cave paintings (*a*, *c*); and from
photographs of dead animals (*b*, *d*). Do (*a*) and (*c*) or (*b*) and (*d*) come
closer to the codes of the original culture?

(*a*) A 'trotting boar'.

(*b*) A slaughtered pig. A composite tracing from two photographs,
with legs in different positions.

(*c*) A 'bellowing bison'.

(*d*) A dead sambur hind.

From Abercrombie (1960)

extend this concept to include aberrant encoding as well. This is encoding
that fails to recognize that people of different cultural or subcultural
experience will read the message differently, and that in so doing they
will not necessarily be blameworthy. The reading of a message does not of
itself include a search for the encoder's intention. Indeed, much fruitless
arguing has occurred, particularly in literary criticism, about the author's
inferred intention.

Arbitrary codes (or logical codes)

Basic concept

These are simply defined, and easily understood. They are codes where the agreement among the users is explicit and defined. They are codes with a stated and agreed relationship between signifiers and signifieds. They are symbolic, denotative, impersonal, and static. Mathematics uses a perfect arbitrary or logical code. No one who has learnt the code can have any disagreement about the meaning of '4 × 7 = 28'. Aberrant decodings are impossible: cultural differences are irrelevant: meaning is not negotiated between reader and text; it is contained in the message. All that is required is to learn the code. Science, the objective, impersonal, universal study of natural phenomena, attempts to communicate its findings in arbitrary, logical codes. Traffic lights, the Highway Code, military uniforms, football shirts, chemical symbols are all further examples.

Further implications

The main differences between arbitrary and conventionally defined codes derive from the different natures of their paradigms. Arbitrary codes have a defined, limited paradigm of signifiers with a precisely related paradigm of signifieds. They emphasize denotative meaning. Conventional codes have open-ended paradigms: new units can be added; existing ones can drop out of use. They tend not to have an agreed paradigm of signifieds. They are thus more dynamic and capable of change. Arbitrary codes are static and can only change by explicit agreement amongst the users.

Arbitrary codes, then, are closed: they attempt to contain the meaning within the text, and do not invite the readers to bring much to their side of the negotiating process. All they require is that they know the code. Conventional codes, on the other hand, are open and invite active negotiation from the reader. Extreme types of conventional codes can be called *aesthetic*, and can sometimes be decoded only via clues within the text.

Aesthetic codes

Basic concepts

Aesthetic codes are harder to define simply because they are more varied, more loosely defined, and they change so rapidly. They are crucially affected by their cultural context: they allow of, or invite, considerable negotiation of meaning: aberrant decodings are the norm. They are expressive; they encompass the interior, subjective world. They can be a source of pleasure and meaning in themselves: style is a relevant concept. Arbitrary logical codes are largely referential; aesthetic codes can perform all of Jakobson's functions.

Further implications

Conventional aesthetic codes acquire their agreement amongst their users from shared cultural experience. Mass art and folk art use conventional aesthetic codes; so do dress and architecture, car and furniture design. They are the codes of the mass society as well as the codes of a traditional tribal society. Frequently, the more conventional or redundant that they are, the more they are called lowbrow and cliché-ridden.

But aesthetic codes can also break conventions as well as follow them: innovative art contains within itself clues or hints towards its own decoding. The artist who breaks with the convention of her or his time hopes society will learn the new codes of his or her work and so will gradually 'appreciate' it. A highbrow work of avant-garde art will frequently use aesthetic codes that are unique to it: the audience must seek within the work itself the clues to its decoding: all that is shared between artist and audience is the work itself. In a mass society, with mass production and mass consumption, the unique work of art acquires an additional status simply because of its uniqueness. It is not available for mass ownership or mass consumption and thus becomes especially highly valued for its ability to signal individual differences and élitist values. This is then translated into high financial value (see Benjamin, 1970).

Conventionalization

There is a common cultural process by which innovative, unconventional codes gradually become adopted by the majority and thus become conventional. This is called conventionalization. This process may involve a highbrow art style, say Impressionism, gradually becoming widely accepted until it becomes the conventional way of painting nature. Or it may involve a narrowcast code, developed for a particular subculture, say jazz, gaining the same sort of broad cultural acceptance. In each case the devotees of the pure or original code will complain that the broadcast version is a degraded one.

Certainly, making a code into a broadcast one involves change: the precise, subtle communication possible when artist and audience share a narrowcast code is neither possible nor proper in a broadcast code. The heterogeneity of the audience will require the code to deal in generalities rather than specific unique meanings, and will allow the aberrant decodings necessary to fit the message into the varieties of convention or cultural experience of the mass audience. We may say these changes are for the worse: that conventionalization involves a lowering of quality because it involves appealing to the 'lowest common denominator'. Such a judgement may be valid, but we should be aware that it is made from within a particular value system, one that values elaborated, narrowcast codes and the expression of individual differences. A value system that rates highly the reinforcement of cultural ties and restricted, broadcast codes will find the metaphor of the lowest common denominator offensive, élitist, and inaccurate.

Codes and conventions

Codes and conventions constitute the shared centre of any culture's experience. They enable us to understand our social existence and to locate ourselves within our culture. Only through the common codes can we feel and express our membership of our culture. By using the codes, whether as audience or source, we are inserting ourselves into our culture and maintaining that culture's vitality and existence. A culture is an active, dynamic, living organism only because of the active participation of its members in its codes of communication.

Suggestions for further work

1. Discuss the role played by codes and conventions in plate 8. Note that the umbrellas are gold, that the 'unnamed' cigarettes are Benson and Hedges 'Special Filter', which have established a gold box as their image, and that a campaign of similar advertisements has 'conventionalized' the surrealist style. What does this tell you about the relationship of codes and conventions to social and communication experience? How important is our experience of other related texts in the decoding of one in particular (that is, intertextuality)? See Guiraud (1975), pp. 40–4; Fiske and Hartley (1978), pp. 61–2.

2. Compare the words of a pop song with a love poem. What light does this shed on the nature of elaborated and restricted codes and on their social function? Undertake the same exercise with reports of the same

MIDDLE TAR As defined by H.M.Government
H.M. Government Health Departments' WARNING:
CIGARETTES CAN SERIOUSLY DAMAGE YOUR HEALTH

Plate 8   *'Raining Cigarettes'*

event in a popular and a quality newspaper. Discuss the difference between value-free analysis and social value judgements. See Hartley (1982), chapters 2 and 10.

3. What are the main differences between arbitrary (or logical) and aesthetic codes? Use Jakobson's model to structure your analysis. See also Guiraud (1975), pp. 45–81.

4. Take one, or more, of Argyle's codes of NVC and attempt to produce a 'vocabulary' for it. What problems do you encounter, particularly those associated with analogue codes? How culture-specific are these

codes? Is it relevant to discuss them in terms of the degree of motivation of their signs? See Guiraud (1975), pp. 88–90; Corner and Hawthorn (1980), pp. 50–61.

5. Turn to plate 4 (pp. 54–5). Discuss the images in terms of the codes they employ. How conventional are they? How aesthetic? Are some broadcast, some narrowcast? Does the medium itself (for example, painting, drawing, photography, cartoon), or the genre within the medium (for example, pornographic, fashion, or personal photography), carry meaning? Or does it identify the appropriate codes – do we decode a painted nude in the same way as a photographed nude?

5 SIGNIFICATION

Saussure's theories on the paradigmatic and syntagmatic relations of the sign take us only so far towards understanding how signs work. Saussure was interested primarily in the linguistic system, secondarily in how that system related to the reality to which it referred, and hardly at all in how it related to the reader and his or her socio-cultural position. He was interested in the complex ways in which a sentence can be constructed and in the way its form determines its meaning; he was much less interested in the fact that the same sentence may convey different meanings to different people in different situations.

In other words, he did not really envisage meaning as being a process of negotiation between writer/reader and text. He emphasized the text, not the way in which the signs in the text interact with the cultural and personal experience of the user (and it is *not* important here to distinguish between writer and reader), nor the way that the conventions in the text interact with the conventions experienced and expected by the user. It was Saussure's follower, Roland Barthes, who first set up a systematic model by which this negotiating, interactive idea of meaning could be analysed. At the heart of Barthes's theory is the idea of two *orders of signification*.

Denotation

The first order of signification is the one on which Saussure worked. It describes the relationship between the signifier and signified within the sign, and of the sign with its referent in external reality. Barthes refers to this order as denotation. This refers to the common-sense, obvious meaning of the sign. A photograph of a street scene denotes that particular street; the word 'street' denotes an urban road lined with buildings. But I can photograph this same street in significantly different ways. I can use a colour film, pick a day of pale sunshine, use a soft focus and make the street appear a happy, warm, humane community for the children playing in it. Or I can use black-and-white film, hard focus, strong contrasts and make this same street appear cold, inhuman, inhospitable, and a destructive environment for the children playing in it. Those two photographs could have been taken at an identical moment with the cameras held with their lenses only centimetres apart. Their denotative meanings would be the same. The difference would be in their connotation.

Connotation

Basic concept

Connotation is the term Barthes uses to describe one of the three ways in which signs work in the second order of signification. It describes the interaction that occurs when the sign meets the feelings or emotions of the users and the values of their culture. This is when meanings move towards the subjective, or at least the intersubjective: it is when the interpretant is influenced as much by the interpreter as by the object or the sign.

For Barthes, the critical factor in connotation is the signifier in the first order. The first-order signifier is the sign of the connotation. Our imaginary photographs are both of the same street; the difference between them lies in the form, the appearance of the photograph, that is, in the signifier. Barthes (1977) argues that in photography at least, the difference between connotation and denotation is clear. Denotation is the mechanical reproduction on film of the object at which the camera is pointed. Connotation is the human part of the process: it is the selection of what to include in the frame, of focus, aperture, camera angle, quality of film, and so on. Denotation is *what* is photographed; connotation is *how* it is photographed.

Further implications

We can extend this idea further. Our tone of voice, *how* we speak, connotes the feelings or values about *what* we say; in music, the Italian direction *allegro ma non troppo* is the composer's instruction about *how* to play the notes, about what connotative or emotional values to convey. The choice of words is often a choice of connotation – 'dispute' or 'strike', 'oiling the wheels of commerce' or 'bribery'. These examples show emotional or subjective connotations, although we have to assume that others in our culture share at least a large part of them, that they are intersubjective.

Other connotations may be much more social, less personal. A frequently used example is the signs of a high-ranking officer's uniform. In a hierarchical society, one that emphasizes distinctions between classes or ranks and that consequently puts a high value on a high social position, these signs of rank are designed to connote high values. They are usually of gold, models of crowns or of laurel wreaths, and the more there are, the higher the rank they denote. In a society that does not value class distinction or hierarchy, officers' uniforms are rarely distinguished from their men's by signs that connote the high value of rank. The uniforms of Fidel Castro or Chairman Mao differed hardly at all from those of the men they led. Yet they were denoted as of high rank just as clearly as was a nineteenth-century Prussian officer who could hardly move under his signs of rank.

Connotation is largely arbitrary, specific to one culture, though it frequently has an iconic dimension. The way that a photograph of a child in soft focus connotes nostalgia is partly iconic. The soft focus is a motivated sign of the imprecise nature of memory; it is also a motivated sign for sentiment: soft focus = soft-hearted! But we need the conventional element to decode it in this way, to know that soft focus is a significant choice made by the photographer and not a limitation of the equipment. If all photographs were in soft focus, then it could not connote nostalgia.

Because connotation works on the subjective level, we are frequently not made consciously aware of it. The hard-focus, black-and-white, inhuman view of the street can all too often be read as the denotative meaning: that streets *are* like this. It is often easy to read connotative values as denotative facts. One of the main aims of semiotic analysis is to provide us with the analytical method and the frame of mind to guard against this sort of misreading.

Myth

Basic concept

The second of Barthes's three ways in which signs work in the second order is through *myth*. I wish Barthes (1973) had not used this term, because normally it refers to ideas that are false: 'it is a myth that . . .' or 'the myth that Britain is still a major world power'. This normal use is the unbeliever's use of the word. Barthes uses it as a believer, in its original sense. A myth is a story by which a culture explains or understands some aspect of reality or nature. Primitive myths are about life and death, men and gods, good and evil. Our sophisticated myths are about masculinity and femininity, about the family, about success, about the British policeman, about science. A myth, for Barthes, is a culture's way of thinking about something, a way of conceptualizing or understanding it. Barthes thinks of a myth as a chain of related concepts. Thus the traditional myth of the British policeman includes concepts of friendliness, reassurance, solidity, non-aggressiveness, lack of firearms. The photographic cliché of a corpulent, jolly bobby patting a little girl on the head relies for its second-order meaning on the fact that this *myth* of the police is common in the culture: it exists before the photograph, and the photograph activates the chains of concepts that constitute the myth. If connotation is the second-order meaning of the signifier, myth is the second-order meaning of the signified.

Further implications

Let us return to our example of the street scene with which we illustrated connotation. If I asked a dozen photographers to photograph this scene of children playing in the street I would predict that most would produce the black-and-white, hard-focus, inhuman type of photograph. This is

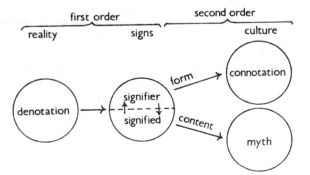

Figure 19 *Barthes's two orders of signification. In the second order, the sign system of the first is inserted into the value system of the culture*

SIGNIFICATION

because these connotations fit better with the commonest myths by which we conceptualize children playing in the street. Our dominant myth of childhood is that it is, or ideally should be, a period of naturalness and freedom. Growing up means adapting to the demands of society, which means losing naturalness and freedom. Towns are normally seen as unnatural, artificial creations that provide a restricted environment for children. There is a widespread belief in our culture that the countryside is the proper place for childhood. We can constrast these myths with those of other periods. For instance, the Elizabethans saw a child as an incomplete adult; the Augustans saw the countryside as uncivilized – the human values were to be found in the civilized cities and the country had to be seen as pastoral, that is made suitable for urban understanding.

Barthes argues that the main way myths work is to naturalize history. This points up the fact that myths are actually the product of a social class that has achieved dominance by a particular history: the meanings that its myths circulate must carry this history with them, but their operation as myths makes them try to deny it and present their meanings as natural, not historical or social. Myths mystify or obscure their origins and thus their political or social dimension. The mythologist reveals the hidden history and thus the socio-political works of myths by 'demystifying' them.

There is a myth that women are 'naturally' more nurturing and caring than men, and thus their natural place is in the home raising the children and looking after the husband, while he, equally 'naturally', of course, plays the role of breadwinner. These roles then structure the most 'natural' social unit of all – the family. By presenting these meanings as part of nature, myth disguises their historical origin, which universalizes them and makes them appear not only unchangeable but also fair: it makes them appear to serve the interests of men and women equally and thus hides their political effect.

The history that these myths turn into nature tells a very different story. These meanings of masculinity and femininity were developed to serve the interests of bourgeois men in capitalism – they grew to make a particular sense of the social conditions produced by nineteenth-century industrialization. This required working people to leave their traditional rural communities and move to the new cities, where they lived in houses and streets designed to accommodate as many people as cheaply as possible. The extended family and community relationships of the traditional village were left behind and the nuclear family of husband, wife, and children was created. The conditions of factory work meant that children could not accompany their parents, as they could in agricultural

89

work, and this, coupled with the absence of the extended family, meant that the women had to stay in the home while the men did the 'real' work and earned the money. The chains of concepts that constituted the related myths of masculinity, femininity, and the family proliferated, but not randomly or naturally: they always served the interests of the economic system and the class which it advantaged – middle-class men. This system required the nuclear family to be the 'natural' basic social unit; it required femininity to acquire the 'natural' meanings of nurturing, domesticity, sensitivity, of the need for protection, whereas masculinity was given meanings of strength, assertiveness, independence, and the ability to operate in public. So it seems natural, but is, in fact, historical, that men occupy an enormously disproportionate number of public positions in our society.

Of course, myths can most effectively naturalize meanings by relating them to some aspect of nature itself. So the fact that women give birth is used to naturalize the meanings of nurturing and domesticity (or 'nest-building'!). Similarly, men's larger and more muscular bodies are used to naturalize men's political and social power (which has nothing to do with physical strength).

The changing role of women in society and the changing structure of the family mean that these myths are finding their position of dominance (and therefore their status as natural) under challenge, so advertisers and the producers of the mass media are having to find ways of triggering off new gender myths which have had to develop in order to accommodate the career woman, the single parent, and the 'new' sensitive man. These myths, of course, do not reject the old entirely, but drop some concepts from their chains, and add others: change in myths is evolutionary, not revolutionary.

No myths are universal in a culture. There are dominant myths, but there are also counter-myths. There are subcultures within our society which have myths of the British bobby contradictory to the dominant one outlined above. So, too, there is a myth of the urban street as a self-supporting community, a sort of extended family that provides a very good social environment for children. This would be the sort of myth to fit with the connotations of our alternative photograph of the street.

Science is a good example where the counter-myths are strongly challenging the dominant. We are a science-based culture. The dominant myth of science presents it as humankind's ability to adapt nature to our needs, to improve our security and standard of living, to celebrate our achievement. Science is seen as objective, true, and good. But the counter-myth is also very strong. This sees science as evil, as evidence of

90

our distance from and lack of understanding of nature. As scientists, we are at our most selfish and short-sighted, in pursuit of our own material ends. It is interesting to note that in popular culture both myths of science are well represented. The factual side of television, news, current affairs, documentaries, tends to show more of the dominant than of the counter-myth; fictional television and cinema, on the other hand, reverse the proportions. There are more evil scientists than good ones, and science causes more problems than it solves.

For example, Gerbner (1973b) shows that scientists portrayed on American fictional television were rated as the most 'deceitful', 'cruel', and 'unfair' of all professional types. He also cites a study in 1963 by Gusfield and Schwartz which again describes the fictional image of the scientist as 'cool', 'tough', 'anti-social', 'irreligious', and 'foreign'. Gerbner also found that scientific research led to murder in nearly half of the twenty-five films which portrayed it. One example was a psychologist who hypnotized gorillas to murder girls who rejected him. A typical plot is an obsessive scientist whose invention gets out of control and kills him, to the obvious relief of the rest of society and the audience.

The other aspect of myths that Barthes stresses is their dynamism. As I said earlier, they change and some can change rapidly in order to meet the changing needs and values of the culture of which they are a part. For instance, the myth of the British bobby to which I referred earlier is now growing old-fashioned and out of date. Its last major fictional presentation on television was in *Dixon of Dock Green*.

Connotation and myth are the main ways in which signs work in the second order of signification, that is the order in which the interaction between the sign and the user/culture is most active.

Symbols

But Barthes (1977) does refer to a third way of signifying in this order. This he terms the *symbolic*. An object becomes a symbol when it acquires through convention and use a meaning that enables it to stand for something else. A Rolls-Royce is a symbol of wealth, and a scene in a play in which a man is forced to sell his Rolls can be symbolic of the failure of his business and the loss of his fortune. Barthes uses the example of the young Tsar in *Ivan the Terrible* being baptized in gold coins as a symbolic scene in which gold is a symbol of wealth, power, and status.

Barthes's ideas of the symbolic are less systematically developed than those of connotation and myth, and are therefore less satisfactory. We might prefer Peirce's terms. The Rolls-Royce is an index of wealth, but a symbol (Peirce's use, not Barthes's) of the owner's social status. Gold is an index of wealth but a symbol of power. Or we might find it useful to leave the Saussurean tradition of linguistics altogether and turn to two other concepts which are widely used to describe aspects of semiosis. These are metaphor and metonymy. Jakobson (Jakobson and Halle, 1956) believes that these two concepts identify the fundamental ways that messages perform their referential function.

Metaphor

Basic concepts

If we say that a ship *ploughed* through the waves, we are using a metaphor. We are using the action of a ploughshare to stand for that of a ship's bow. What we are doing is expressing the unfamiliar in terms of the familiar (the metaphor assumes that the ploughshare's action is familiar, that of the ship's bow is not). The jargon terms are 'vehicle' for the familiar, 'tenor' for the unfamiliar.

One further characteristic we must note is that a metaphor exploits simultaneous similarity and difference. Thus we can say it works paradigmatically, for vehicle and tenor must have enough similarity to place them in the same paradigm, but enough difference for the comparison to have this necessary element of contrast. They are units with distinctive features in a paradigm. Thus the metaphor 'ploughed' is in the paradigm of verbs meaning 'to cleave'. So the metaphor works like this:

Literal: The ship |*moved* through the water.
Metaphoric: |*ploughed*
                       |*sliced*
                       |*cut*
                       |*chopped*
                       |*cleaved*
                       |*etc.*

paradigmatic choice

What is happening, then, is a process of metaphoric transposition:

Tenor: The ship   *moved* through the water.
            ↑   ↑   ↑
Vehicle: The ploughshare*ploughed* through the earth.

92

⟶ Metaphoric transposition of *ploughed* to *moved*.

------→ Associated transposition when other characteristics of the vehicle are transposed by association. Characteristics of the ploughshare, such as its powerful, relentless heaviness are transposed to the ship; similarly, characteristics of the earth are transposed to the water.

Further implications

This is the traditional literary definition of a metaphor. When we transfer our attention from arbitrary signs to iconic signs we encounter a few problems.

Metaphors are rarer in visual languages and we will better understand why after our discussion of metonymy (below). It is sufficient to say here that the visual language that most frequently works metaphorically is that used by advertisers. Often an event or object is set up as a metaphor for a product. Mustangs in the Wild West are a metaphor for Marlboro cigarettes; waterfalls and natural greenery are a metaphor for menthol cigarettes. These are clear, manifest metaphors in which both vehicle (mustangs and waterfalls) and tenor (cigarettes) are visually present. Even here, the *difference* is played down though obvious. But there is currently a style of surrealist advertisements which approximate much more closely to verbal metaphors, in that the difference is exploited as much as the similarity (plate 8, p. 83). This is a visual version of the metaphor 'It is raining cigarettes'.

Everyday metaphors

But metaphors are not just literary devices: Lakoff and Johnson (1980) have shown that they have a much more fundamental, everyday function. They are part of the way in which we make sense of our everyday experience. Let us take two examples.

When we talk about 'high' morals, 'falling' asleep, or the 'lower' classes we are talking metaphorically and using the same metaphor each time: in this the spatial difference between UP and DOWN is made to act as the vehicle for a variety of social experiences. It is a concrete, physical difference that is used to make sense of a number of more abstract, social experiences. This difference, though natural, is not neutral: we humans think that one of our key distinctions from other animals is that we have 'risen up' on our hind legs as part of the 'upward' evolutionary process. So UP always has positive values attached to it. The differences between social classes, for example, could be thought of horizontally, from left to right, but is actually thought of vertically, from higher to lower. So, too, artistic taste is called 'high' or 'low' brow, and the 'higher' brows go with the 'higher' classes (and vice versa), as do 'higher' earnings and a 'higher' social profile. UP is also associated with consciousness and health (we wake 'up', but 'fall' asleep or ill) and with the dominant system of morality – 'high' morals. When we add to this the realization that the gods are 'up' in heaven, the devils 'down', and that life itself is 'up' (Christ 'rose' from the dead) and death 'down', we can begin to understand how fundamentally such an everyday metaphor influences the way we think.

We use the single metaphor of UP:DOWN to make sense of a wide range of diverse social abstractions such as god, life, health, morals, social position, earnings, and artistic taste, and in linking them together it works ideologically (see chapter 9). There is nothing *natural* that links high social position, high earnings, and high morals, but making sense of them through the same metaphor is one way in which the dominant values are spread throughout society.

The second example is that of using money as a metaphor for time. When we talk of 'saving' or 'wasting' time, or of 'investing' time in a project, we are thinking of it as money. Of course, time is very different from money – it cannot be saved, one person cannot collect more of it than another, and it cannot be invested to produce more of itself. Using money as a metaphor for time is typical of the social values that we call 'the Protestant work ethic': the metaphor implies that any time that is not related to working productively (which includes 'earned' leisure) is 'misspent' – particularly time 'spent' doing nothing or in indulging our pleasures. The metaphor is a way of disciplining our thinking in a way that is appropriate to, and part of, the ideology of a work-centred, capitalist society.

Both these metaphors are examples of what Lévi-Strauss calls 'the logic of the concrete' (see chapter 7). He claims that all societies make sense of abstractions that are important to them by metaphorically embodying them in concrete experience. These concrete metaphors, such as *up* or *money*, then become 'tools to think with': they form and shape our understanding of those abstractions and thus enable us to handle them conceptually in our everyday lives.

Such everyday metaphors differ from literary metaphors in a number of ways. They do not draw attention to themselves as metaphors, and thus do not invite us to decode them consciously. They are thus more insidious, and the sense that they make becomes more easily part of our society's 'common sense'; that is, it becomes part of the uninspected, taken-for-granted assumptions that are widespread throughout society.

Such common sense appears to be natural, but it never is: it is always arbitrary, always socially produced. It is, then, finally, ideological: the power of the dominant classes is maintained partly to the extent that their ideas can be made into the *common* sense of all classes. It is ideological common sense, for example, that leads blue-collar workers to see their social position as 'lower' than that of managers; it is ideological common sense that makes us think of having fun as wasting time. Everyday metaphors are more ideological and covert than literary ones, and so we need to be all the more alert to them and the 'common' sense they are making.

Metonymy

Basic concepts

If metaphor works by transposing qualities from one plane of reality to another, metonymy works by associating meanings within the same plane. Its basic definition is making a part stand for the whole. If we talk of the 'crowned heads of Europe' we are using a metonym. For Jakobson, metonyms are the predominant mode of the novel, while metaphors are that of poetry. The representation of reality inevitably involves a metonym: we choose a part of 'reality' to stand for the whole. The urban settings of television crime serials are metonyms — a photographed street is not meant to stand for the street itself, but as a metonym of a particular type of city life — inner-city squalor, suburban respectability, or city-centre sophistication.

The selection of the metonym is clearly crucial, for from it we construct the unknown remainder of reality. On a recent television programme, *The Editors*, two shots of picket lines were shown. One was of an orderly group of men standing outside a works while two of them spoke to a lorry driver; another was of a group of workers violently struggling with the police. The point is that both shots were of the same picket line on the same day. The second, of course, was the one shown on the news that night. The selection of metonym determines the rest of the picture of the event that we construct, and trade unions frequently protest that the metonyms given in the news lead the viewer to construct a very one-sided and incomplete picture of their activities.

James Monaco (1977) shows how metonyms are used in film. For instance, a shot of a weeping woman's head beside a pile of banknotes on a pillow is a metonym of prostitution: he sees a gesture or pose as a metonym of the emotion it expresses.

Further implications

Metonyms are powerful conveyors of reality because they work indexically. They are part of that for which they stand. Where they differ from the 'natural' indexes, like smoke for fire, is that a highly arbitrary selection is involved. The arbitrariness of this selection is often disguised or at least ignored, and the metonym is made to appear a natural index and thus is given the status of the 'real', the 'not to be questioned'. But all news films are metonyms and all involve this arbitrary selection. Only one of the two shots of the picket line was transmitted on the news and the choice of which was to be transmitted was made on two sets of criteria. The first are those of news values. Galtung and Ruge (1973) have shown that the dominant news values in this country are such that an event is more likely to be reported if:

(a) it concerns élite personalities;
(b) it is negative;
(c) it is recent;
(d) it is surprising.

The second are those of cultural values, or *myths*. Our dominant myth of the trade unions is that they are disruptive, aggressive, hostile to the wider good of the nation, and are generally negative organizations. Clearly the second shot 'fitted' the dominant myth, and the news values. It had to be the one selected.

Metonyms, myths, and indexes

Fiske and Hartley (1978) have shown in detail how myths operate in news broadcasts. Myths work metonymically in that one sign (for example of the jolly British bobby) stimulates us to construct the rest of the chain of concepts that constitute a myth, just as a metonym stimulates us to construct the whole of which it is a part. Both are powerful modes of communication because they are unobtrusive or disguised indexes. They exploit the 'truth factor' of a natural index and build on it by disguising its indexical nature. We are aware that smoke is *not* fire, or that black clouds are *not* a thunderstorm; but we are not aware in the same way that a shot of a picket line is not *the* picket line, or a shot of a bobby is not *the* police force. The disguising extends also to the arbitrariness of the selection of the sign. Other signs of a policeman or a picket line would activate other myths; other metonyms would give other pictures of reality. The main aim of semiotic analysis is to strip off this disguise.

Metonyms, myths, and indexes all work in similar ways in that the signs and their referents are all on the same plane: they work by contiguity. There is no transposition involved as with metaphors nor any explicit arbitrariness as with symbols. Hawkes (1977) suggests that metonyms work syntagmatically. We can add myths and indexes to this in so far as all three require the reader to construct the rest of the syntagm from the part given by the sign.

Metaphors and paradigms

Jakobson argues that metaphor is the normal mode for poetry, whereas metonymy is the normal mode for the realistic novel. The previous section has discussed why 'realism' is necessarily a metonymic mode of communication and has thus provided reasons for the comparative rarity of metaphors in representational art or photography, both of which are realistic. Metaphor is not essentially realistic, but imaginative: it is not bound by the principle of *contiguity* on the same plane of meaning; instead it demands, by the principle of *association*, that we seek similarities between manifestly different planes. It requires imagination to associate a ploughshare with a ship's bow.

More artistic, obscure metaphors require more imaginative effort from the reader. 'I have measured out my life with coffee spoons' requires considerable imagination from the reader to associate characteristics of coffee spoons with means of measuring time: coffee spoons (metonyms for 'drinking coffee' as a social, superficial 'tinkling' act) take on associations of regularity and repetition, together with a sense of being the most significant event in one's life. Associating cigarettes with rain involves the same work of imagination.

This principle of association involves transposing values of properties from one plane of reality or meaning to another. This transposition takes place between units in a paradigm (for example, the ship ploughs, cuts, slices, etc., or I have measured out my life with birthdays, winters, times I've lost my job, coffee spoons, etc.) and metaphor therefore works paradigmatically. It is from this that metaphor derives its imaginative, poetic effect, because normal paradigms can, by imagination, be extended to include the new, the surprising, the 'creative'. Thus the normal paradigm of 'ways of measuring time/life' can be extended to include 'coffee spoons'. Or we can imaginatively create a special paradigm that includes 'cigarettes' and 'raindrops': one of long, thin, round objects normally seen in quantity. Other possible units in the paradigm could be 'matchsticks' (too close to cigarettes to exploit the quality of difference needed for this sort of original metaphor), 'trimmed logs awaiting transport from the forest', or 'bundles of drainage pipes on a building site'. Both those last are possible imaginative paradigmatic choices for metaphors for cigarettes.

So metonyms work syntagmatically for realistic effect, and metaphors work paradigmatically for imaginative or surrealistic effect. It is in this sense that connotation can be said to work in a metaphoric mode. Reading soft focus as sentiment involves an imaginative transposition of properties from the plane of feelings to the plane of construction of the signifier. Soft focus is a metaphor for sentiment. A dissolve is a metaphor for the act of memory. Gold buttons in the form of crowns and gold braid are metaphors for the high social status of a general's rank. But these connotations are constructed rather than true metaphors, in that although they involve the imaginative transposition of properties from one plane to another, they stress the similarity between the planes and minimize the difference.

Suggestions for further work

1. Changing the type-face of a word is a good example of changing the signifier. So type-faces should all have connotations. Collect examples of various type-faces and discuss their connotations.

   Produce words or phrases in different type-faces, and try to control or predict their connotations (use Letraset if your graphic ability is limited). see chapter 8 and question 4 for the use of the semantic differential — you can use this to check the accuracy of your predictions.

2. There are a number of myths of the British police, as indicated by the variety of terms used to refer to them — bobbies, cops, the fuzz, pigs, filth. Try to identify for each term both its associated myth and the subculture for which it would be valid. Return to plates 1a and 1b and analyse them in terms of myth and connotation.

   How does this exercise help you understand the way in which a myth is validated from two directions — its truth to reality, and the extent to which it meets the needs of its user culture? See Barthes (1973), pp. 114–21, and Hartley (1982), chapter 2.

3. Analyse the advertisement in plate 9. Discuss the metaphoric transpositions in it. What are the devices by which it makes the snake and the drink members of the same paradigm? (Note that in the original the drink in the glass and the snake are the same shade of yellow.) You should compare the Barthesean and the more

Plate 9   *'The Snake in the Glass'*

traditional meanings of the term myth – and how it relates to
symbols. Why do you think the advertisers have tried to convey their
meaning metaphorically rather than literally? What other second-
order meanings are activated? See Williamson (1978), pp. 17–24.

4.   The edition of *The Editors* mentioned in this chapter also showed
shots of musicians picketing the BBC during a musicians' union
strike. There was not a policeman in sight; the strikers were good-
humoured, and played to a crowd that quickly collected; they were
supported by scantily-clad dancing girls; their spokesman was
cultured, articulate, and middle-class. The whole piece had a jokey

tune. Discuss this in terms of myth, metonym, and news values. How does it relate to more 'normal' portrayals of (a) picket lines, (b) musicians? How far does our understanding of the piece rely on the defeat of our expectations of normality?

6 SEMIOTIC METHODS AND APPLICATIONS

'A Grief Ago': poetic metaphor

A Grief Ago is the title of a poem written by Dylan Thomas. G. N. Leech (1969) gives a good example of how semiotic/linguistic methods of analysis can give us some insight into how this phrase gains its poetic power. The four concepts of paradigm, syntagm, norm, and deviation can go a long way towards explaining this particular phrase.

Norms and deviation

A norm is a statistically average example of behaviour or evaluation. It describes the common practices of a group or society and is thus *predictable*, the expected. Widely accepted *conventions* are close to the norm. The unexpected, the non-conventional is a *deviation* from the norm. To be accurate we ought to envisage a scale with the norm at one end and extreme deviation at the other; there are degrees of normality and degrees of deviation. In practice, however, it is tempting, if misleading, to talk of the normal and the deviant as if they were distinct categories. If we do this, we must remember that the line between them is constantly on the move; frequently this movement is inwards, towards the central, normal position. Long hair for men was deviant, then became much more normal; trousers for women, or calling older people by their Christian names, or omitting the full stops after initial letters are other examples of deviant behaviour becoming normal.

Paradigm and syntagms

'A Grief Ago' is a deviant use of language in that the syntagm:

A . . . . . AGO

is normally completed by one of a set of words with particular characteristics, that is, words from a particular paradigm. In this case the characteristics of the normal paradigm are:

(a)   words concerned with the measurement of time;

(b)   words concerned with regularly recurring events;

(c)   words with a plural form.

So we can construct a paradigm sharing degrees of normality or deviance to complete the syntagm A . . . AGO (see figure 20). I have given a rough order of deviation, but it is only rough and will vary for different people. Those at school may find that 'A lesson ago' is more normal than 'A moon ago'; Hollywood film stars may find that 'Three wives ago' is more normal than 'Three winters ago'. But the principle of degrees of deviation, rather than hard-and-fast categories, is what matters.

The word 'grief' is deviant in all three characteristics. It normally belongs in a very different paradigm and is thus normally found in very different syntagms. By inserting it into this particular syntagm, Dylan

Norm	Word	Paradigmatic characteristic		
		Time	Recurrence	Plurality
	Minute	+	+	+
	Hour	+	+	+
	Week	+	+	+
	Month	+	+	+
	Etc.			
	Moon	−	+	+
	Winter	−	+	+
	Game	−	+	+
	Lesson	−	+	+
	Cigarette	−	+	+
	Overcoat	−	+	+
	Wife	−	−	+
	Etc.			
	Grief	−	−	−
Deviation	Nature	−	−	−

Figure 20   *Verbal paradigm*

Thomas has temporarily given it the characteristics of its new paradigm, while retaining those of its original one — that of major emotions. By investing grief with the characteristics of measuring time, regular recurrence, and plurality, he has given the word a new set of meanings that many readers find particularly apt or imaginatively pleasing. Creativity or originality frequently means breaking norms or conventions and semiotic analysis can help us to understand what norms are being deviated from, to what extent, and, possibly, to what effect.

Pasta: visual metaphor

The same process can often be seen in visual texts, particularly advertisements. The advertiser will often take advantage of the technical scope of photography to 'insert' or 'superimpose' objects normally in one syntagm into another. There is an advertisement for a brand of pasta (plate 10) which shows a place setting: in the centre of the plate, where the food normally goes, is a wheat field in brilliant sunshine. Where the norm would lead us to expect prepared food cooked by artificial heat, we see natural raw food warmed only by the sun. The syntagm of 'dinner plate with . . . on it' would normally be completed by a unit from the paradigm with the characteristics of cooked, artificial, taken away from nature. It *is* completed, however, by a unit from the paradigm of the natu al, the healthy. Another cereal uses a verbal equivalent of this paradigmatic switch in its slogan 'The Sunshine Breakfast'.

Both Dylan Thomas's phrase and the pasta advertisement are working metaphorically, in that they are taking units from one paradigm and inserting them into a syntagm which would normally be completed by units from another. By so doing they are associating the characteristics of the two paradigms in a new and imaginatively striking way by the process of transposition (see p. 92). All metaphors are, in this sense, deviations from the norms of language behaviour. What can happen, and frequently does, is that a metaphor becomes so common, so frequently used, that it becomes the norm. This is when it becomes a cliché and loses its original imaginative impact.

The examples given have shown us that these transpositions can be in both directions. We can say that 'grief' acquires more from the paradigm with which it has been associated than it brings with it from its normal one. 'Ploughed' (see p. 92) and the pasta advertisement, however, bring more from their normal paradigm than they gain from their new one. It is this sort of imaginative work involved in metaphoric or paradigmatic transpositions than lies behind Jakonson's belief that poetry works mainly

Plate 10   *'Pasta Plate'*

by metaphor whereas realism works mainly by metonym. Constructing a picture of reality from a metonym requires a different sort of imagination than does the ability to associate normally distinct paradigms.

Notting Hill: realistic metonym

We can extend our semiotic analysis by moving in this direction. A news photograph introduces a new set of problems for the analyst. It is iconic, and not arbitrary, so the paradigms involved are less well specified than

104

they are in a verbal syntagm. It works metonymically, not metaphorically, and so does not draw attention to the 'creativity' involved in its construction: it appears more 'natural'. Plate 11a is a photograph taken at the 1976 Notting Hill Carnival in London, part of which turned into a confrontation between young blacks and police. Plate 11b is the use that the *Observer* made of it.

First-order syntagm

At the denotative level, the first order of signification, plate 11a causes few problems. It is a syntagm made up of a number of visual signs. One of the problems of analysing iconic syntagms, like this, is that the signs combined into it are not distinct and clearly separable as they are in arbitrary syntagms like sentences. Barthes refers to this when he calls a photograph 'an analogue' of reality. None the less, I think I can see two main, and three subsidiary, signs in it; I think, therefore, that I can see digital distinctions in an analogic code. Further analysis will be able to break these signs down into their components, just as the grammatical analysis of a sentence can proceed into more and more detailed levels of analysis. Each sign here is like a phrase in a sentence.

The two main signs are the group of black youths and the group of policemen. The three subsidiary signs are the crowd of blacks surrounding the incident, the urban setting – underside of a flyover and

Plate 11a   *Notting Hill*

old terraced houses – and the tree. The syntagm brings these signs into a particular relationship – one of a confrontation that is connected in some way, possibly causal, to the urban, black setting. Certainly the confrontation is not independent of its environment.

These signifiers on the page become signs when we read them, that is when we match them with signifieds or mental concepts. We have concepts of the police, of blacks, of the inner city, and of trees which we need to read this picture. These signifieds are the result of our cultural experience: we can recognize the uniformed figures as policemen and not, say, a Salvation Army band: our signified of the blacks takes account of our knowledge that blacks are comparatively recent, noticeable immigrants into a predominantly white society.

Second-order syntagm: myth and connotation

Once we start thinking about the signifieds, we realize how unreal the distinction is between the first and second orders: it is of analytical convenience only. For the signifieds slide imperceptibly into the second-order myths.

The photograph inevitably triggers off our existing chain of concepts that forms our myth of the police. This picture works through the dominant myth: the police are not aggressive (despite the batons): one shields his face with his arms defensively; two have their backs to the youths; one has been knocked over and has lost his helmet. The signified of the black youths draws on two myths: that of the blacks, and that of disaffected youth. So the confrontation is both one of race, and one of the generation gap: the forces of law and order or society or *us* are set against the forces of anarchy, the antisocial, and *them*. The confrontation in the photograph becomes, at this level, a metonym of internal stress and conflict within our society at large. The myth of the inner city is at work here too. The underside of a flyover is a metonym of a run-down problem area at the centre of a big city. The crowd of blacks in the background shows that this is their neighbourhood. But these 'readings' can only be properly made in the context of our knowledge that the city is in a white liberal democracy and is, like its police force, run by whites.

The *Observer* has cropped this photograph. It has changed its shape, made it long and narrow, so our eyes swing from left to right as we look at it. This reinforces the connotations of confrontation: the movement of the reader's eyes becomes an iconic representation of the exchanges between the two sides. The tree, the only potential softening influence, has gone. But the underside of the flyover remains (the picture could have

Plate 11b   *Observer Review*

been cropped to the top of the leading black's head) and the black crowd remains. Four words have been added, in heavy black print, placed to separate the two main protagonists. The words themselves, their position, and the type-face all underline the connotations of this conflict.

The professional's view

Harold Evans (1978), then the editor of *The Times*, commented that this picture 'was the result of perceptive picture editing as well as of resourceful photography'. The uncropped version, he continued, 'also registered trees and houses and background which added nothing to the news, and, if left in, would have taken publication space from the main focus of attention. There is plenty of detail as well as drama in what remains and at the size and shape reproduced it took every reader by the eyeball.'

It is interesting to see how the professional's reasons compare with a semiotic reading. Shannon and Weaver's concept of noise can explain part of Evans's reasons for the cropping, but he was also concerned with the news values of drama and detail, and with the technical and economic matters of publication space. He approaches the semiotician's concern when he talks of taking the reader by the eyeball. The difference between the two, however, is that the professional assumes that the effect upon the reader is determined largely, if not exclusively, by the photograph itself: the reader is seen as the receiver of the message, upon whom, if the communication process has been efficiently conducted, the effect will be considerable. Harold Evans assumes the basic model of the process school.

107

The semiotician gives a more important role to the reader. The image certainly plays some part in producing its meaning, but so, too, does the reader. The impact, or 'eyeball grabbing', is largely determined by the fact that the reader already has a level of concern and a range of social attitudes about the incident and the social relationships of which it is a metonym. The structure of the text has to interact with the social attitudes of the reader for impact to occur. The difference between the two schools is one of proportionate emphasis, not of irreconcilable alternatives.

The mythologist's view

Cropping out the depressed urban environment is a way that the editor, however unintentionally, is helping perform myth's function of naturalizing history. It closes off the possible meaning that the conflict was caused by social deprivation and prefers the one that black youths tend 'naturally' to be disruptive, aggressive, and anti-social. Such a white myth of blackness is used to explain the fact that blacks occupy a disproportionate number of places in the courts and jails of white societies by reference to their nature instead of their social conditions. The myth denies the history of slavery and colonialism in Caribbean and African countries which lies behind both the presence of blacks in Britain and their disadvantaged social position. It denies, also, the more recent history of insensitive over-policing in black neighbourhoods which is part of the events in the picture. The words YOUNG BITTER AND BLACK help this naturalizing process by suggesting that the bitterness is caused by their 'nature' as black youths, and not by their treatment by a white society.

Barthes is clear that the normal function of myths is to serve the interests of the dominant classes. White interests are well served by these racist myths because they allow whites to avoid recognizing that it is their history and their position of privilege, not the nature of blacks, that has produced the bitternes and disorder of the events in the photograph. The myths wrongly centre the problem and its solution in the black sector of society rather than the white. Demystifying them by a mythological analysis is thus a social and political act. Meanings are never just textual; they are always socio-political, and it is upon this dimension that the mythologist focuses.

Paradigms

In verbal or arbitrary languages, the paradigms are clearly defined, and alongside the paradigms of signifiers is a paradigm of signifieds. Iconic languages, like photography, work differently: there is a potentially infinite number of photographs of the police. But, as Saussure reminds us, any one unit in a paradigm must be significantly different from the rest. So, the infinite number of photographs of the police is a problem only in the first order of signification. In the second order there is a limited number of significantly different 'ways of photographing the police'. There are comparatively few values or emotions to be connoted, and even fewer myths by which we understand the police force. There is a second-order paradigm here, one of myths and connotations. The paradigm may not be explicit as in an arbitrary code, but there is none the less an unspoken consensus within our culture of the dominant units in it.

One interesting question that arises from this is whether other cultures, or subcultures within our own society, have the same paradigm of 'ways of photographing the police'. If they do not, then the second-order meanings that they read will change. This photograph might connote to us the value of police restraint and tolerance; to others it might connote police weakness or even fear; to yet others it might connote police intrusion or intervention. This problem of different readings, particularly in the second order, is one that we will return to at the end of this chapter. For the moment I wish to remain with paradigmatic analysis and to introduce a useful method. This is known as the commutation test.

The commutation test

The commutation test has two main functions. The first is to identify significant differences, or distinctive features, within a paradigm or syntagm; the second is to help us define that significance. The technique involves changing a unit in the system and assessing the change in meaning, if any, that has occurred. Normally the change is made imaginatively, and the meaning of the changed syntagm assessed the same way. Thus we can imagine that the van on the right of the syntagm was changed into a car. And I think we would agree that this would make no difference to the meaning of the photograph. The van is not a signifying unit. Or we could imagine that the background was changed into a prosperous white suburb. This would radically alter the meaning of the syntagm. Instead of seeing the conflict as an inner-city one, unpleasant but confined, contained, we would be led to see it as a far more widespread, threatening one, spilling out into society at large. Or imagine that everyone in the photograph was white, or that the group of blacks were respectably dressed middle-aged men.

Admittedly, in the news photograph these choices are hypothetical. The photographer obviously did not choose a group of black youths in preference to one of white men. But the reading of the photograph involves the recognition that these are *not* white, *not* middle-aged, *not* middle-class people. The commutation test helps us to establish the meaning of this group by identifying what it significantly is not.

Of course, when we analyse advertising photographs, we know that the choices have been deliberate: the photographer will be aware of them in the way that the news photographer almost certainly is not. This is much more akin to the editorial choices involved in the words YOUNG BITTER AND BLACK. Commute the form of these words to normal print and place them outside the frame, in a more normal position for a caption, or imagine they were changed to BLACK BITTER AND YOUNG. Or imagine them in white, printed on the group of policemen and changed to THE BESIEGED BRITISH BOBBY. All these commutations are significant and would change the meaning of the whole.

Words and image

This brings us to a comparison of the roles of words and pictures. Barthes (1964) uses the term *anchorage* to describe the function of words used as captions for photographs. Visual images, he argues, are polysemous: 'they imply, underlying their signifiers, a floating chain of signifieds, the reader able to choose some and ignore others'. Words help *'fix* the floating chain of signifieds in such a way as to counter the terror of uncertain signs'. It is true that we rarely, if ever, see a photograph without some verbal caption, if only one that tells us, at the denotative level, where or of what it is. Elsewhere Barthes (1961) calls the caption a 'parasitic message designed to connote the image, to quicken it with one or more second-order signifieds'. He recognizes that connotation gives the reader a greater range of possible meanings than does denotation, and that words can be used to narrow this range or to close off parts of it.

Another function of anchorage is what Barthes calls *denomination*. This tells us simply what the photograph is of, and thus helps us to locate it accurately within our experience of the world. Telling you that this photograph is of 'the Notting Hill Carnival' helps you place it and thus *anchor* its meanings. I could have said it was of race riots in Smethwick or of Cardiff City football supporters leaving the ground or of the shooting of an episode of *Dixon of Dock Green*: each of these *denominations* would have closed off certain meanings and led you towards others.

Preferred readings

At the second order, then, the words direct our reading. They tell us, sometimes, *why* the photograph was considered worth taking and frequently *how* we should read it. They direct us towards what Stuart Hall (1973b) has called 'a preferred reading'. In this case, the preferred reading is one that guides us to a meaning of the photograph that lies within the traditional values of law and order. These values are faced with an urgent problem, but the problem is capable of solution within them. In other words, the preferred meaning *closes off* potential revolutionary meanings of the photograph. We are not encouraged to negotiate a meaning that includes the idea that the social structure is wrong, unjust, and needs to be physically overthrown. Such meanings are, of course, possible and are even predictable for a minority group in our culture. But they are not preferred: they would be *aberrant decoding* (Eco, 1965). This preferred meaning links the 'race problem' to the 'youth problem' or 'generation gap' – one that is familiar and which we know causes stresses and strains, but which does not pose a fundamental threat to society itself. The potential linking of 'race' to 'class', a far more explosive link, is *closed off* from us by the words.

This notion of preferred reading is a fruitful one for it gives us a model that enables us to link the negotiated meanings of a message with the social structure within which both message and reader operate. Hall derives and elaborates this notion from Parkin. Parkin (1972) argues that there are three basic meaning systems by which individuals interpret or respond to their perception of their condition in society. These systems he calls the dominant, the subordinate, and the radical. Stuart Hall suggests that these correspond to ways of decoding mass-media messages.

The *dominant system*, or *dominant code*, is one which conveys the dominant values, the preferred readings of the society. The dominant definition in this photograph is that the police are our representatives, maintaining our free society, and that young blacks who challenge this role must be seen as 'deviant' or criminal.

The *subordinate system* corresponds to what Hall calls the *negotiated code*. This accepts the dominant values and existing structure, but is prepared to argue that a particular group's place within that structure needs improving. This may be a union negotiating better wages for its members, or it may be a white liberal 'negotiating' a better place for blacks in our society. This negotiated decoding of the photograph might include accepting that while the police in general perform their function efficiently and correctly, they can be faulted in their dealings with blacks. In certain aspects of their role, we might say, they are repressive agents of

111

the dominant majority keeping subordinate or deviant elements firmly in their place: this may be no bad thing when they are dealing with the criminal underworld, but is morally wrong when they treat blacks in the same way.

Hall's *oppositional code* corresponds to Parkin's *radical system*. This reading rejects the dominant version and the social values that produced it. The oppositional decoder recognizes the preferred reading but rejects it as false. He or she locates the message in a meaning system that is radically opposed to the dominant one, and therefore negotiates a radically opposed reading of the text. An oppositional reading of this photograph will be that it shows the blacks' natural expression of their rights and freedom being forcibly held down by the agents of the ruling class. This is a metonym of an unjust social system at work.

These analyses of the second-order meanings of the photograph have brought us to the concept of *ideology*. The preferred meaning of this photograph can be arrived at only within the values of a white, liberal, democratic ideology. I shall reserve full discussion of ideology for chapter 9.

Social determination of meaning

Hall and Parkin have shown that what readers bring to their negotiation with the text is determined by their place in the social structure; both believe that social class is what primarily determines this place. Morley (1980) has followed up their ideas with an empirical investigation of audience readings of two editions of the television programme *Nationwide*. His findings broadly support the Hall/Parkin position, but show that social class by itself is not the determinant that Hall and Parkin assume it to be. Thus groups of apprentices (working-class) and bank managers (middle-class) both gave dominant readings, whereas university students (middle-class) and trade-union officials (working-class) both gave (different) negotiated readings. Oppositional readings came from blacks who rejected the programme as totally irrelevant, and shop stewards who radically opposed it.

Morley has shown that the model really does work, but that we must recognize that social forces other than class help to determine the negotiating position of the reader. These factors may include education, occupation, political affiliation, geographical region, religion, or family. Each of these produces a *discourse*, a register of languages with its attendant ways of conceptualizing the world. So an individual has a number of discourses deriving from the various social groupings of which

Plate 12 *'Mr Honda'*

s/he is a member: reading is a negotiation between the numerous discourses of the reader and the discourse in the text.

Suggestions for further work

1. The analysis of 'A Grief Ago' is typically Saussurean in that it sees the language system as the site of meaning; the analysis of the Notting Hill photograph relates the symbolic system to the social system. Discuss the relative merits of each approach. Choose a poetic metaphor (or simile) and a news photograph to analyse.

2. How closely do the notions of norms and deviation fit with those of convention and originality, and of redundancy and entropy? Can our earlier discussion of the communicative functions of redundancy help us understand 'A Grief Ago' and how and with whom it communicates? Is the poet a communicator?

3. Is there any difference between the poet's use of language and the advertiser's who describes tight skirts as 'stem-slim classics of lethal grace . . . panther sleek and fabulously disciplined' (Dyer, 1982)? Should we search for any difference in the aesthetic quality of the language itself, in its social function, in its referential 'truth', or where? How aesthetic is advertising in general? Is it art? See Dyer (1982), chapters 2 and 7.

4. Give a full, detailed semiotic analysis of plate 12. (Note that the sun rising on the left is, predictably, red.) Apply to it the theory of preferred readings. See Barthes (1977), pp. 15–31, 32–51, but especially pp. 20–5, and (1973), pp. 116–21.

5. Return to plate 1b. Analyse the way that the words are trying to 'fix' the possible meanings of the photographs. Using the same photographs, produce new layouts and headlines for:
   (a) a black community newspaper;
   (b) *Police Gazette*;
   (c) a Moscow newspaper.
   Further reading: Hall, in Cohen and Young (1973), pp. 176–89, and in Hall *et al.* (1980), pp. 136–9; Fiske and Hartley (1978), chapter 3 and pp. 103–5; Morley (1980), pp. 10–11, 16–21, 134; McKeown (1982).

7 STRUCTURALIST THEORY AND APPLICATIONS

Semiotics is a form of structuralism, for it argues that we cannot know the world on its own terms, but only through the conceptual and linguistic structures of our culture. Empiricism (see chapter 8) argues exactly the opposite. For the empiricist the work of the researcher is to discover the meanings and patterns that already exist in the world; for the structuralist the task is to uncover the conceptual structures by which various cultures organize their perception and understanding of the world. While structuralism does not deny the existence of an external, universal reality, it does deny the possibility of human beings having access to this reality in an objective, universal, non-culturally-determined manner. Structuralism's enterprise is to discover how people make sense of the world, not what the world *is*. Structuralism, therefore, denies any final or absolute scientific truth — if universal unchanging reality is not accessible to human beings, then we cannot evaluate the truth of statements or beliefs by measuring how closely they approximate to this reality.

This is often a difficult idea to grasp for it contradicts the scientific rationalism that has dominated western thought since the Renaissance. Lévi-Strauss (1979) distinguishes between 'scientific' and 'savage' ways of thinking, not to assert that scientific thinking is better, but that it is different. It works by establishing differences; it divides nature up into ever finer and more precise categories. 'Savage' thinking, on the other hand, is holistic; it attempts to find ways of understanding all of nature, not bits of it. It thus encompasses areas of experience that science rules out as unreal or unscientific, so matters of belief, imagination, and subjective experience do not count as part of its reality. Of course, western science is more instrumental in its power to change the world than the magical explanations of phenomena in some tribal societies. But a religious 'truth' may be effective in working to change people's attitudes and behaviour; it may affect our social and political systems; and it may offer apparently 'truer' explanations of subjective experiences than empirical science can. Truth is a function of the conceptual and cultural system that makes it and accepts it: it is not a function of a universal, objective, pre-cultural reality.

Lévi-Strauss was a structural anthropologist who extended Saussure's theory of language as a structural system to cover all cultural processes, such as those of cooking, dressing, kinship systems, and especially myths and legends. These are all ways of organizing and therefore making sense of our cultural and social worlds. All cultures make sense of the world, and while the meanings that they make of it may be specific to them, the ways by which they make those meanings are not; they are universal. Meanings are culture-specific, but the ways of making them are universal to all human beings.

Thus, for Saussure, all languages are different: their vocabularies divide the world up into quite different categories; their syntaxes link concepts in quite different ways. But all of them are arbitrary; all of them share the same paradigmatic and syntagmatic structure: all of them, paradigmatically, rely upon a system of categories whose meaning depends on their relationship to other categories in the same system, and all of them have systems of combining categories to make original 'statements'. All languages, therefore, share a structure of differences and combination.

Categorization and binary oppositions

For Lévi-Strauss the paradigmatic dimension of language, that is its system of categories, was the more important. Making conceptual categories within a system was, for him, the essence of sense-making, and at the heart of this process was the structure that he called a *binary opposition*. A binary opposition is a system of two related categories that, in its purest form, comprises the universe. In the perfect binary opposition, everything is either in category A or category B, and by imposing such categories upon the world we are starting to make sense of it. So category A cannot exist on its own, as an essential category, but only in a structured relationship with category B: category A makes sense only because it is not category B. Without category B there could be no boundary to category A and thus no category A. Structurally, the story of the creation in Genesis can be read not as the story of the creation of the world, but of the creation of cultural categories by which to make sense of it. The dark was divided from the light, the earth from the air. The earth was divided into categories of land and water, and water divided into waters of the sea (infertile) and of the firmament, or rain (fertile). This last shows us an example of the second stage of the sense-making process, when categories that apparently exist in nature, that is categories that correspond very closely to our perception of concrete reality, are used to explain more abstract, more generalized, and more apparently culture-specific concepts, and to ground these explanations in nature and thus to make them appear natural and not cultural. So the opposition of the apparently natural categories of sea water and rain water is used to explain and naturalize the more abstract and culture-specific categories of infertile and fertile. This process of making sense of abstract concepts by metaphorically transposing their structure of differences on to differences of the concrete that appear to be natural is, according to Lévi-Strauss, a common cultural process; he calls it 'the logic of the concrete'. So, later on in the Genesis story, the grasses are divided into leaf-bearing and seed- or grain-bearing, and this distinction is used to help think through the much more problematic distinction between humans and animals: humans eat the grain-bearing grasses and animals eat the leafy ones.

The construction of binary oppositions is, according to Lévi-Strauss, the fundamental, universal sense-making process. It is universal because it is a product of the physical structure of the human brain and is therefore specific to the species and not to any one culture or society. The brain works electrochemically by sending messages between its cells, and the only messages it can send are simple binary ones of ON/OFF. Such is the complexity of the network that the human brain, like its electronic homologue the computer, can construct incredibly sensitive systems of categories by an almost infinite number of refining repetitions of these binary oppositions. (This process has been described in the section on 'bits' of information in chapter 1.) The difference between digital and analogue codes (see chapter 4) is that digital codes are built upon a system of opposed categories.

But nature is not: nature is a series of analogic continua, rather than neat categories. In nature there is no dividing line between light and dark but a continual process of lightening and darkening; there is not even a clear line between land and water — the beach, quicksands, mud are all categories that resist neat binary oppositions. These categories, ones that partake of characteristics of both the binarily opposed ones, Lévi-Strauss calls *anomalous categories*.

Anomalous categories

An anomalous category is one that does not fit the categories of the binary opposition, but straddles them, dirtying the clarity of their boundaries. Anomalous categories draw their characteristics from both of the binarily opposed ones, and consequently they have too much meaning, they are conceptually too powerful. Their excess of meaning which is drawn from both categories and their ability to challenge the basic sense-making structures of a culture means that they have to be controlled – typically by being designated 'the sacred' or 'the taboo'. Anomalous categories derive from two sources – nature and culture. Nature always finally resists the categorization that culture tries to impose upon it. There are always bits of nature that intransigently refuse to fit. Thus, to return to our Genesis example, the snake is neither a beast of the land nor a fish of the sea, but has characteristics of both. Therefore, in a Judaeo-Christian culture, it has too much meaning, it is semiotically too powerful, and thus has to be controlled by being made taboo. Similarly, homosexuality threatens the clarity of the gender categories, and in a society such as ours where gender identity is so crucial, it is surrounded with all sorts of taboos, both moral and legal.

The other type of anomalous category is one constructed by the culture itself to mediate between two opposed categories when the boundary appears too stark, too terrifying. Thus many cultures mediate between gods and people by means of anomalous figures (angels, Jesus Christ) who partake of both. Similarly, there are numerous mythological or religious figures who mediate between humans and animals (werewolves, centaurs, and sphinx) and between the living and the dead (vampires, zombies, ghosts).

Structured repetition

Because the structuring principal is the fundamental way of making sense of our world, structuralism seeks parallel structures that organize apparently quite different parts of our cultural existence in similar ways. Leach (1964), for example, finds parallels in the way we conceptualize our spatial environment, our relationship to animals, and our relationship to people. He traces parallel categories with parallel anomalies between them. Let me simplify his analysis to bring out its main points.

Space is categorized into 'the house', 'the farm or neighbourhood', and 'the wilderness'. Animals fit into parallel categories – 'pets', 'farm animals', and 'wild animals'. People are similarly categorized into 'family', 'our tribe/neighbours', and 'the others/aliens'. But these categories, of course, are not always adequate, particularly in the last two cultural areas. So animals that live in the house, but are neither pets nor farm animals, are vermin, taboo, and endowed with excess meaning – rats and mice are especially repulsive to many people. The equivalent category in human relationships is that of step-relatives, who are neither family nor tribe, but have characteristics of both. Leach points out how the stepmother is typically a taboo figure, occupying the category in the human world that in the animal would be occupied by vermin.

Similarly, between farm and wild animals lies an anomalous category occupied by foxes (in Britain), coyotes (in the US), and dingoes (in Australia). They are wild, but they hang around farms and houses and have some characteristics of domestic animals, particularly dogs. The human equivalent is 'criminals', who are a mixture of characteristics of 'our tribe' and of 'the others/aliens'. Leach again notes how typical it is for foxes, coyotes, and dingoes to be given criminal roles and attributes in folk stories: they are typically thieves and confidence tricksters.

There is also a set of structural parallels between the edibility of the animals and the marriageability of the humans. Pets are not to be eaten, family members cannot be married; farm animals are normally eaten, marriage partners normally come from within the tribe/neighbourhood; wild animals are eaten only on special occasions, and can be killed only by 'licensed' people at 'licensed' times – all societies distinguish between those who may and those who may not hunt, and many have specific hunting seasons. Game (which is a wild edible animal) is an especially festive meal. So, too, marriage between persons from different tribes happens only on special occasions – often to form political alliances – or with great concern for its abnormality, as in inter-racial marriages in our society. Similarly, animals in the anomalous categories are not normally eaten; nor are people in the equivalent categories considered as good marriage partners.

This is another typical example of the logic of the concrete, when the apparently natural categories of space and of animal species are used to naturalize and justify first the more cultural categories of kinship, and second the highly culture-specific and more abstract categories of edibility and marriageability.

Boundary rituals

Structural anthropologists argue that the vital importance of boundaries between categories has produced in all societies a series of boundary rituals designed to ease the transition between them. In general, the bigger the categories that are being transgressed, the more elaborate and important the ritual. Thus all societies have rituals to give meaning to the passages between living and not living, whether this passage be that of birth or death. Similarly, the passages between single and married, or between childhood and adulthood, typically have elaborate rituals to mark and make sense of the crossing of the categorical boundaries. The much less elaborate and everyday rituals of greetings and departures mark the boundaries between presence and absence.

These passages between categories are often marked by anomalous periods – the honeymoon, the mourning and viewing of the body in the coffin, the period between birth and christening – which are sacred because they are neither one category nor the other: they have traces of the one that has been left and foreshadowings of the one that is to follow. They are periods that help members of the society to adjust their meanings of the altered person so that the transition is not so abrupt as to be disorientating.

Similarly on television, credit and title sequences or station identifications are forms of boundary ritual. They enable the viewer to adjust between the changing categories of, say, quiz shows and the news, or the news and a soap opera. Title sequences typically foreshadow the category of programme that is to follow – title sequences for the various news programmes are quite different in kind from those for soap operas, which differ in their turn from those for action dramas. Without these boundary rituals, television's flow of different programme categories would be more confusing. Similarly, a honeymoon makes it easier for people to adjust to the new categorical status of the married couple. Opening and closing sequences can also be seen as television's equivalent of greeting and leaving rituals.

The importance of marking some of the categorical boundaries on television is recognized in Britain by the requirement that programmes and advertisements must be clearly separated by a blank screen or a symbol. In the US no such requirement exists, and programmes and commercials can easily blur into each other. The confusion of the viewer that results is, of course, to the advantage of the advertiser, who wishes to maintain the 'willing suspension of disbelief' with which a viewer watches a favourite drama programme, and does not want it replaced by the cynicism and distancing that is more appropriate to commercials. The choice of which boundary crossings to mark by rituals and which to ignore can tell us quite a lot about the priorities of a society – in Britain greater priority is given to the viewer/consumer, in the US to the advertiser/producer.

Nature and culture

Lévi-Strauss believed that one of the crucial boundaries that all societies try to make sense of is that between nature and culture. Culture is a sense-making process that makes sense not only of external nature or reality, but also of the social system that it is part of, and of the social identities and daily activities of the people within that system. Our sense of ourselves, of our social relationships, and of 'reality' are all produced by the same cultural processes.

But most cultures do not recognize the continuity between making sense of ourselves and a society and making sense of reality or nature: instead they draw a clear distinction between nature and culture, and try to use the meanings or categories that appear to them to be inherent in nature itself to make sense of more obviously cultural conceptualizations. There is a double, contradictory movement here: cultures differentiate themselves from nature in order to establish their own identity, and then legitimate that identity by comparing it back to nature, and establishing it as 'natural' rather than cultural. Nature, then, is the raw reality that surrounds us; however inaccessible in its own terms, 'the natural' is the sense that a culture makes of nature: the natural is a cultural product, nature is pre-cultural reality.

In his book *The Raw and the Cooked* (1969) Lévi-Strauss analyses the significance of food and cooking as cultural processes, and then extends this so that it acts as a metaphor for a far wider range of cultural transformations. Food is a particularly powerful anomalous category, for it constantly crosses those vital categorical boundaries between nature and culture, between me and not-me, the internal and the external worlds. So moments of key cultural significance are nearly always marked by ceremonial eating, and the cooking process by which raw food is transformed into cooked culture is one of the most important cultural processes. This process starts conceptually before any instrumental transformation, for all cultures divide nature into the 'edible' and the 'non-edible', though all, of course, place different natural objects in each category. The human stomach is capable of digesting almost anything, so the distinction between the edible and the non-edible has no physiological basis, only a cultural one. The significance of this distinction is evidenced by the frequency with which the difference or alienness of another society is identified by its designation of something as edible that we consider inedible. So Frenchmen are known to the English as frog-eaters, and Scots as haggis-eaters; Arabs are aliens because they eat sheep's eyes, and Aboriginals because they eat witchetty grubs.

This conceptual transformation of nature into culture (its categorization into the inedible and the edible) becomes the technical process of cooking. All human societies cook their food, though, again, the human stomach is capable of digesting it raw. Cooking is a cultural transformation, not a material necessity. Lévi-Strauss's elaborate analysis of cooking systems is an extreme example of structuralist methodology, and shows some signs of strain (for a good simple account of it see Leach, 1970), but, for our purposes, his most significant distinction is between boiling (or frying) on the one hand, and roasting (or grilling) on the other. He also distinguishes between these as highly cultural ways of transforming food, and the more natural one of rotting. Broadly, he argues that there is an inverse relationship between the degree of cultural transformation and the social value given to the resulting food. So boiled food is highly cooked − it requires both utensils and an agent such as water or oil. It is also 'democratic' in that it increases the amount of food. Roasting, on the other hand, is 'aristocratic' − it wastes food by shrinking it, and it transforms it less because it requires only heat and not mediating utensils and agents. So roast meat is commonly given a high valuation, and is eaten by high-status members of a society, or on high-status occasions. Boiled or stewed meat, conversely, is given a low valuation, is eaten by low-status members of society (especially women, invalids, and children), and is more of an everyday food than a special one. Rotted food has often the highest status of all because it is the least transformed, the most natural; so Stilton cheese and well-hung game are particularly aristocratic tastes in our society.

While we can obviously find exceptions to Lévi-Strauss's account at the level of detail, at the broader level it is useful in explaining a basic cultural transformation, and in drawing attention to the relationship between the degree of transformation and the social status of the resulting product.

The structure of myth

For Lévi-Strauss, a myth is a story that is a specific and local transformation of a deep structure of binarily opposed concepts that are important to the culture within which the myth circulates. The most powerful and significant myths act as anxiety reducers in that they deal with the contradictions inherent in any structure of binary oppositions, and, although they do not resolve them (for such contradictions are often finally irreconcilable), they do provide an imaginative way of living with them, and coping with them so that they do not become too disruptive and do not produce too much cultural anxiety.

Lévi-Strauss's theory of myth owes at least as much to Freud as it does to Saussure. From Saussure he developed his emphasis on the paradigmatic structure of binary oppositions (see below) and his argument that each telling of the myth — which will necessarily differ from other tellings — can be best understood as a form of *parole*, a particular realization of the potential of the deep structure (or *langue*). As the Saussurean linguist studies various *paroles* (which are all there is to study) in order to arrive at the underlying structure of *langue*, so the mythologist studies the various versions of a myth (which are also all that is available for study) in order to arrive at its deep structure.

From Freud he develops the idea that the analysis of myth is the cultural equivalent of the analysis of the dreams of an individual. A dreamer will know that he or she is dreaming, but will know only the dream's (often absurd) surface meaning: its deeper, 'real' meaning is available only to the analyst. So, too, the teller of myth will know only its surface meaning: the 'real' meaning embodied in its deep structure is available only to the analyst. As dreams arise from anxieties and unresolved traumas that have been repressed in the subconscious of the individual, so myths arise from the repressed anxieties and unresolved contradictions hidden in the tribal or cultural subconscious. Myth analysis, then, is very similar to dream analysis, though it uses a structuralist methodology because its concern is with culture-specific meanings rather than individual-specific ones.

A simple example will make this clearer. Lévi-Strauss (1979) retells a North American myth in which humans and animals were not clearly differentiated. The villain of the myth was the South Wind, which was so strong and cold as to make normal activities impossible when it was blowing. So the beings (humans and animals) set out to capture it and tame it. The successful hunter was the skate (a large flatfish) who negotiated the wind's release on the condition that it agreed to blow only on alternate days, thus leaving ones when the beings could go about their normal business. This myth is handling the opposition between the benign and hostile sides of nature, but what fascinates Lévi-Strauss is the choice of the skate as hero. He explains it by arguing that alternate absence and presence of the wind is given material form in the skate, for the skate when viewed from the side is almost invisible (absent) but when viewed from above or below is enormous (present). By the 'logic of the concrete', the skate embodies the opposition between hostile and benign nature, the presence and absence of the wind, and thus mediates between them. The structure of the myth can be modelled as in figure 21.

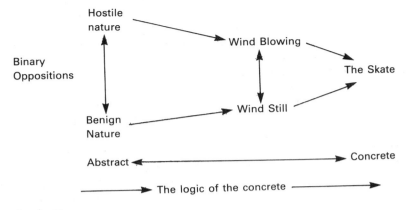

Figure 21

The final meaning of the myth, then, lies not in its narrative or syntagmatic structure, for the events of the expedition and actual hunt are comparatively superficial decorations and do not *need* retelling. The final meaning is to be found in the paradigmatic relationship of opposed concepts which is a conceptual way of structuring and thus of making sense of the real problem. The paradigmatic relation of hostile to benign nature is transposed metaphorically on to the equivalent paradigm of the presence or absence of the wind: the paradigmatic difference is then collapsed into the skate, which contains the difference in a final unity – it is, after all, a single being. Each paradigmatic shift is therefore a metaphoric transposition away from the abstract towards the concrete – the wind is a concrete metaphor for the hostility or benignity of nature, the skate a concrete metaphor for the wind's absence or presence.

The myth analyst, then, uses Saussurean and Freudian methods to arrive at the deep problems that concern a society and the way that myths structure and mediate these problems, and circulate their ways of thinking throughout the society.

The structure of mass culture

In industrial societies, the mass media are often considered to perform a function equivalent to that of myth in tribal, oral ones. So Lévi-Strauss's theories can be applied to the contemporary mass media, in both their fictional and factual modes. Thus all the episodes of a television series may be seen as various *paroles* of its deep structure or *langue*. This may be extended, too, so that each example of a genre may be seen as a particular

124

realization of the potential of its deep structure. Viewed in this way, all westerns would be specific versions of the same myth of The Western, or, to put it another way, the same deep structure of binarily opposed concepts can generate an infinite number of individual westerns. So, too, the deep structure of a television series can generate an infinite number of episodes, or the deep structure of a tabloid front page can generate an infinite number of possible headlines and pictures. This is an exact parallel to the way that a *langue* can generate an infinite number of *paroles*. Let us apply this in two slightly different ways, by analysing first an individual western, *The Searchers*, and then the cover of a tabloid.

Application 1: 'The Searchers'

The Searchers opens with a shot of an isolated homestead in the barren landscape of the Wild West. Its opening shots are dominated by 'the domestic', the details of everyday life performed largely by women and children. Then, through the open door of the homestead, we are shown a distant figure of a horseman in the landscape. He approaches, dismounts, is met by the family, and we learn that he is Uncle Ethan (played by John Wayne), who has been absent for many years. He is invited in, and joins the family at supper. During the meal another horseman appears in the distance, also seen through the open door of the homestead; he gallops up and dismounts by an Indian rather than a white way, that is by swinging his leg over the horse's neck rather than its rump. He joins the family at the meal, and is met by a hard stare from Ethan, and the comment (which in the 1980s would be unacceptably racist): 'I could mistake you for a half-breed.' We learn that he is Mark, one of whose great-grandparents was a Cherokee.

These first few minutes of the film have set up the structure of binary oppositions that underlie the whole narrative (and the western genre). The rest of the narrative concerns an Indian attack upon the homestead, the kidnapping of the young daughter Lucy, and the subsequent search for her by Ethan and Mark, who eventually rescue her and restore her to her family and a happy marriage. The opening shots emphasize the binary opposition of the homestead and the landscape, which is quickly established as a concrete transformation of the more abstract oppositions between the developed East and the 'raw' West, between whites and Indians, between law-and-order and anarchy, between humanity and cruelty, and, more problematically, between femininity and masculinity, between society and the individual. Finally, of course, the deep structured opposition is that between culture and nature. The meanings

Indoors : Outdoors
The Homestead : The Landscape
The Family : The Individual
Women (and children) : Men
Whites : Indians

Law and Order : Anarchy
Peace : War
Civilization : The Primitive Savage
Christianity : Paganism
Femininity : Masculinity
Progress : Stagnation
THE EAST : THE WEST

Humanity : Cruelty
Fertility : Barrenness
Safety : Danger
Education (Knowledge) : Ignorance
Good : Evil

CULTURE : NATURE

Metaphoric transpositions from abstract to concrete: the logic of the concrete

Anomalous or Mediating characters: Hero (Ethan)
Anti-Hero/Helper (Mark)

Figure 22

that derive from this opposition are, of course, ones pertinent to a white, patriarchal, capitalist, imperialistic, expansionist society that sees nature as a raw resource to be colonized and exploited to the full. We may model the structure as in figure 22.

There are a number of points to make about this structural analysis. Although it is primarily derived from the study of one myth only, it depends upon our knowledge of other myths in the genre, if only at the level of cross-checking the categories, for it cannot be valid if it is not capable of generating every other western myth. Of course, each western story need not refer specifically to every binary opposition – the schoolmarm (education:ignorance) is often absent, though the sheriff (law-and-order:anarchy) is almost always present, and the preacher (Christianity:paganism) is frequently included.

I have divided this structure into three main groups of values. The first is of concrete, actual elements in this particular narrative. The second is of the values specific to white patriarchal capitalism which are given concrete form in the first group and which give the elements of that first group their culture-specific meanings – which, in fact, enable the concrete details to operate mythically, beyond the level of specific instances. This second group can be contained within the meanings of THE EAST and THE WEST (of the US). The third group consists of values which apparently belong to a universal and therefore natural value system, that of the morality of GOOD:EVIL and the way it is manifest in local instances. These are realized in the more culture-specific values of the second group and, in their turn, work to naturalize them, that is to appear to locate them in nature rather than culture. It is, of course, important to realize that this third group of values are finally culture-specific, but they have been given the status of 'the natural' and thus can be made to appear to be part of nature rather than culture.

This structure, then, shows how the actual objects and events of a narrative relate to its deep structure in two directions. First, they act as real and therefore unchallengeable examples of more abstract and therefore problematic cultural concepts: they ground the abstract in the concrete, the cultural in the natural. Second, they are themselves given significance by their relationship with the deep structure of abstract and broad cultural categories: they are moved out of the random and into the structured, and thus out of the meaningless and into the meaningful. We know what the objects, people, and events of the narrative *mean* (even if not consciously), and much of our pleasure in the narrative derives from our awareness of the structure (and thus the meaning system) into which they have been inserted. There is, then, a constant two-way movement up and down the structure, between the concrete and the abstract, between the surface and the depth, that is characteristic of all mythic narrative.

But this structure is not without its problems. A culture that wholeheartedly embraced the values of the left-hand side of the diagram and totally denied those of the right would seem sterile and boring, and would, in some way, lack the motivation for development. Thus, to take a simple example, capitalism depends upon risk-taking: it cannot work if people play for safety all the time. Similarly, its competitiveness demands a degree of cruelty, of lack of concern for the loser. In the narrative the Indians are crueller than the whites, but in reality white society, in its racial imperialism, has been far crueller to the Indian than vice versa. The problems with the simplicity of this structure are most sharply focused around the categories of 'masculinity' and 'the individual'.

The immediate contradictions are that, here, masculinity and the individual appear on the negative side of the structure, whereas in a patriarchal, bourgeois capitalist culture they should appear on the positive side. But, of course, the values on the negative side of the structure are not unrelievably so, just as those on the other side are not unrelievably positive. The concepts of masculinity and the individual need some of the wildness, the ruthlessness, the amorality of nature: too much civilization, too much of the social, can be debilitating or feminizing. So, while the role of the feminine in the western may be typically that of socializing or taming the masculine, this is never seen as uncontradictorily good or positive. Hence the need for the anomalous western hero, such as those played by John Wayne, who combines many values from each side of the structure. He is an individual who operates on the side of society (but who always rides away as a free loner back into nature as the final credits roll); he comes out of the landscape into the homestead, and returns to nature and the sunset at the end of the narrative. He is at home in nature like the Indian; he is both savage and civilized, both primitive and developed, both 'Indian' and 'white'. The hero is so mythically powerful and narratively successful because he draws his semiotic strength from both sides of the structure. The hero mediates the contradictions between nature and culture: he does not resolve them, for they are finally irreconcilable, but he embodies a way of managing them and of structuring them that is pertinent to a particular society at a particular time. John Wayne mediates these contradictions for the 1950s and 1960s as Clint Eastwood does, quite differently, for the more cynical 1970s and 1980s. The change in the western hero is part of a change in society's meanings of progress, of imperialism, of capitalism, of good and evil.

Application 2: the mythic structure of the 'Weekly World News'

Lévi-Strauss frequently takes apparently unrelated myths from apparently unrelated tribes and demonstrates that the same deep structure underlies them; he concludes, not that myths travel easily and one tribe borrows myths from another, but that common anxieties and problems about the relationship between culture and nature, humans and gods, death and life, us and them, and so on must produce a deeply structured set of binary oppositions which are common, and which therefore generate myths whose differences are merely superficial. It is a theory and a methodology that seeks an organizing unity underneath an apparent diversity.

The cover of the *Weekly World News* (plate 13) is, on first glance, a collection of unrelated stories, but a closer look reveals a deep structure underlying them. The two lead stories allow us to probe into this structure. The scientific proof of the existence of the soul and of life

Plate 13   *Weekly World News*

after death is a structurally similar story to the tears on Elvis's painting: they both share the deep binary opposition of LIFE:DEATH, and the more culture-specific, and therefore less deep, oppositions into which this is transformed. These include those of science:religion, rationality: irrationality, mundane:miraculous, Christianity:paganism, and natural: supernatural. A number of interesting points emerge from this preliminary analysis. The first is that these oppositions are used to question and undermine the socially dominant values, not to support them. In a rationalist but avowedly Christian society such as ours, the relationships between science and religion are necessarily fraught and our society tries to keep the two domains as separate as possible; but when they do come into direct conflict, science is normally given the greater value – for example in the creation–evolution debate, or in the cases of those whose religion forbids blood transfusions or medical treatment. In these stories, however, we are positioned to believe the experiences and explanations which lie beyond science's power to produce the 'true' facts – for 'truth' is, of course, a social construct and its production and circulation is central to the exercise of power in society. Scientific truths may not be 'better' than religious truths, but they do have far greater social acceptability and power.

So 'science' normally refuses to accept the existence of the soul, as it refuses the 'truth' that pictures may cry. These stories contradict the dominant norms; one invites us to side with 'abnormal' science (and Christianity) against normal science, and the other to side with pagan superstition against Christianity. In each story, we take the side of the unofficial or less powerful 'knowledge'. The fact that Christianity changes sides (it is less socially powerful than science, but more powerful than paganism) is unimportant – the structural relationship between the more and less legitimate 'truths' remains the same, and this is what matters to structuralism. Any one unit can change its place in a system according to the other units to which it is related without disturbing the structure of the system. So 'Christianity' can change its position from 'less socially powerful' (in relation to science) to 'more socially powerful' (in relation to paganism). The story of the tears on Elvis's picture opposes Christianity, because Christianity proposes the truth that such 'miracles' are confined to God, Christ, and saintly people – a category that does not normally include pop stars.

The stories of the psychic making the river run backwards and of the (possible) space aliens in our ancestry also share the common structure – the normal versus the abnormal, scientific reason versus the inexplicable. So, too, if less obviously, does that of the 'cheatin' hubby', for here reason and science are embodied in the laws of probability, whereas coincidence and chance are products of an inexplicable system lying beyond rationality.

The two more everyday stories (the mom rescuing her niece and the girl swimming herself to death) are still concerned with matters of life and death, though at the physical rather than the spiritual level, and with socially dominant norms. Each is seen as abnormal. The gun-toting mom rescuing her niece from a kidnapper inverts the social norms of the masculine and feminine, and of the public (or the official) and the private (or the individual). She is performing functions normally reserved for men and the police; she is doubly disempowered (by being a woman and a private individual) yet succeeds against the social norms. This story questions the social norms by inverting them. The other questions the norms by exceeding them. Sport is officially encouraged because it promotes socially desirable values, so a story in which the norms of 'gutsy' endeavour (in sport or work) are exceeded to the point of death calls them into question. The story tells us that the girl worked too hard for her coach, with an implicit parallel to the worker working (too) hard for her or his boss. Excess always questions the normality of that which is exceeded. This whole front page is excessive, and its excessiveness invites an enjoyable scepticism, so that our disbelief of the 'official' experiences and explanations overspills on to the *Weekly World News* itself – we are as sceptical of these stories as we are of the social norms they are exposing.

This page, then, performs a mythic function for the disaffected and disempowered in contemporary America. The social norms and the values that they carry are embodied in such powerful concepts as science, reason, and the natural, and are challenged by less legitimated values which appeal to the subordinate if only because they offer ways of questioning the social system that disadvantages them. One way of coping with a social system that disadvantages one is by disbelief, a general scepticism in which everything is taken with a grain of salt. The mythic structure underlying the diverse stories on this page then, would look like figure 23.

The political and social import of this structure lies in the relationship of the deep 'universal' oppositions of CULTURE:NATURE and DEATH:LIFE with the more socially and historically specific ones into which they are transformed. This relationship is the reverse of what one might expect, in that the positive concepts of NATURE and LIFE are aligned with the weak and disadvantaged. The social system that disempowers them is shown to be unnatural and inadequate, and the values it disparages are shown to be the more positive and the more 'true' because they are closer to a sense of nature that our society denies in the name of scientific reason.

131

Science : Religion
Rationality : Irrationality
The Explicable : The Inexplicable
Christianity : Paganism
The Mundane : The Miraculous
The Natural : The Supernatural
The Physical : The Psychic
Probability : Coincidence
(over-) Exertion : (normal) Effort
Masculine : Feminine
The Public : The Private
Official : Individual
The Powerful : The Weak

Culture/Society : Nature
Death : Life

Figure 23

Myth and social values

Analysing the *Weekly World News* in this way pushes Lévi-Strauss's ideas into an area where he never ventured — that of social differences, particularly, but not exclusively, those of class. These are more central to Barthes's theories of myth, though, again, our analysis contradicts Barthes's central definition of myth in capitalist societies, which is that, with very few exceptions, it promotes and serves the interests of the dominant classes.

In most ways Barthes's and Lévi-Strauss's theories of myth are diametrically opposed. For Lévi-Strauss myth is a narrative that is recognized as a myth even if its meanings are not consciously negotiated by the people using it. For Barthes myth is an associated chain of concepts: people may well be conscious of the meanings of this chain, but not of its mythic character. Myth, for Barthes, disguises its very operation and presents its meanings as being natural; for Lévi-Strauss, its operation is open, its meanings are what is hidden.

For Barthes myth is class-based: its meanings are constructed by and for the socially dominant, but they are accepted by the subordinate, even if they go against their interests, because they have been 'naturalized'. Lévi-Strauss sees myth as dealing with anxieties and problems shared by the whole society, and, ultimately, by the human race. His neglect of class difference may well be explained by his material, which is the myths of tribal societies, whereas Barthes is concerned with those of late-twentieth-century capitalist ones.

Both theorists see myth as a form of language, a way of circulating meanings in society, but their differences appear here as well. Barthes sees language as class-dominated – for him linguistic resources are no more equally distributed than economic resources; and he focuses as much on speech (*parole*) as on language (*langue*) – because he is just as concerned with how language is used as with the abstract potential of its system. Lévi-Strauss, on the other hand, is more interested in the systems by which language structures all our thought and meanings. He is more purely Saussurean in his rejection of history and social specificity as more superficial and thus less significant than the non-historical, universal nature of the system itself. Barthes tends to take this for granted, and lays his emphasis on the historical and social uses to which the system is put. Lévi-Strauss grounds his argument on the structure of the human brain, Barthes on the structure of capitalist societies. But neither of them were directly concerned with the politics of gender and racial differences.

The analysis of the *Weekly World News* reveals a myth of the subordinate, and thus extends the theories of both Lévi-Strauss and Barthes. It also shows that subordination is linked to gender as well as class. When we follow up the stories, this link becomes stronger. The coach who pushed the female swimmer to her death was male; it was women who saw Elvis's tears on his picture. Capitalist societies are also patriarchal ones: men benefit from both economic power and gender power. Reading myth is reading social values, but these values do not serve all members of society equally, and thus in patriarchal capitalist societies the mythologist explores the role played by meanings in the distribution of power in society, and that power is both class-based and gender-based.

Structuralism teaches us to look for the deep structures that underlie all cultural and communication systems. It also enables us to demonstrate that the various social and cultural systems that we use to organize and make sense of our lives are not random or disconnected, but are analogous to each other. (The social system of patriarchal capitalism is analogous to the structure of *The Searchers* – and to that of the western genre – as it is to the structure of the *Weekly World News*.) It therefore places communication (that is, the social generation and circulation of meaning) at the centre of any society. Language, myths, and symbolic systems are the focus of structuralists' attention, for they provide unique insights into the way a society organizes itself and the ways its members have of making sense of themselves and of their social experience.

Suggestions for further work

1. Take a Clint Eastwood western and analyse it structurally as *The Searchers* was analysed in this chapter. Which of the pairs of binary oppositions are common to both movies? Have the terms in any of them changed places? Can your comparison of the two structures help to account for the differences between the heroes typically played by John Wayne and Clint Eastwood? Kottak (1982) has a structural comparison of *The Wizard of Oz* and *Star Wars* which you may find useful as a model.

2. Analyse the page from *Seventeen* (plate 16, p. 179) in the way that the page of the *Weekly World News* was analysed here. What does the comparison of the two enable you to deduce about their different readerships and their social situations?

3. Compare Barthes's and Lévi-Strauss's theories of myth. Can the two be combined or are they irreconcilable? Take an example of contemporary culture and apply each theory to an analysis of it; compare your findings.

4. Use structuralist methods to analyse a popular place as a cultural text. Typical places might include the beach, a camp site, a shopping mall or department store, a national monument, a park. Fiske, Hodge, and Turner (1987) and Fiske (1989b) give some helpful examples.

8 EMPIRICAL METHODS

We have now outlined the basic theory of semiotics and structuralism, and illustrated their applications. Semiotics is essentially a theoretical approach to communication in that its aim is to establish widely applicable principles. It is concerned with how communication works, with the systems of language and culture, and particularly with the structural relationship of semiotic system, culture, and reality.

It is thus vulnerable to the criticism that it is too theoretical, too speculative, and that semioticians make no attempt to prove or disprove their theories in an objective, scientific way. It can also be criticized on the grounds that the evidence used to support or illustrate the theories is highly selective. I chose the examples in chapter 6, critics would say, because they gave untypically clear illustrations of the theories I was expounding. And further, how can I know that the readings I have discussed do, in fact, take place? Can I be sure that I have offered anything other than my personal subjective and thus possibly idiosyncratic decoding?

Empiricism

These critics would argue that semiotics does not have an empirically validated base of evidence upon which to rest its theory. The aims of empiricism are: to collect and categorize objective facts or data about the world; to form hypotheses to explain them; to eliminate, as far as possible, any human element or bias from this process; and to devise experimental methods to test and prove (or disprove) the reliability of the data and the hypotheses.

Empiricism differs fundamentally from semiotics in that:

(a) it is deductive instead of inductive;
(b) it assumes a universal, objective reality available for study;
(c) it assumes that humans are able to devise methods of studying this reality objectively;
(d) it assumes that hypotheses explaining this reality are capable of proof or disproof.

It does, in other words, fit neatly with the common-sense, science-based picture of the world that our western technological materialist society is based on. This is not the place to go into the relative merits of deductive empirical and inductive theoretical ways of understanding reality. What I wish to do in this chapter is to show some empirical ways of approaching areas similar to those covered semiotically in the last few chapters. The first of these is content analysis.

Content analysis

Content analysis is designed to produce an objective, measurable, verifiable account of the manifest content of messages. It analyses the denotative order of signification. It works best on a large scale: the more it has to deal with, the more accurate it is. It works through identifying and counting chosen units in a communication system. Thus if I watch all television drama over a period and count the numbers of men and women portrayed, I will find that men outnumber women by at least 2:1. This is a content analysis. The units counted can be anything that the researcher wishes to investigate: the only criteria are that they should be readily identifiable and that they should occur frequently enough for statistical methods of analysis to be valid.

Kennedy and Nixon

Words are often counted. Paisley (1967) counted the number of times Kennedy and Nixon used particular words in their four television debates during the 1960 election. Their use of the words 'treaty', 'attack', and 'war' showed interesting differences. The data in table 2 provides some evidence for the conclusion that Nixon's attitude was more bellicose, Kennedy's more conciliatory.

Content analysis must be non-selective: it must cover the whole message, or message system, or a properly constituted sample. It is in explicit contrast to more literary forms of textual analysis which select

Table 2   *Kennedy and Nixon: word frequency*
Frequency of use per 2500 words

Word	Kennedy	Nixon
Treaty	14	4
Attack	6	12
War	12	18

particular areas of the message for special study while ignoring others. It claims a scientific objectivity.

Women on television

This can be a useful check to the more subjective, selective way in which we normally receive messages. For instance, we may *feel* that women get a raw deal on television. Content analysis will enable us to provide some objective check on this.

Seggar and Wheeler (1973) studied job stereotyping in American fictional television and found that women were shown in a far more restricted range of occupations than were men (see table 3).

Dominick and Rauch (1972) found the same occupational stereotyping in a study of advertisements. The jobs portrayed may have differed; the similarity was that women still had a far more restricted range of occupations than men (see table 4). They also noted that women in advertisements were essentially home-bound creatures: they were portrayed indoors twice as often as outside, and five times as often as in a business setting. Only 19 per cent of their portrayals were outdoors, whereas 44 per cent of male portrayals were.

Gerbner and Gross (1976) found that women were far more likely than men to have a family, romantic, or sexual matter as their primary role in television drama. They found, for instance, that:

one in three male leads are or intend to get married;
two in three female leads are or intend to get married;
one in five males are in the sexually eligible age-group;
one in two females are in the sexually eligible age-group.

Content analysis can also be used, perhaps paradoxically, to study the form as well as the content. For instance, Welch *et al.* (1979) compared the style of television commercials for toys for boys with that of commercials for girls' toys. They found that advertisements for boys were more 'active' in that there were more cuts, and therefore more shots per

Table 3 *Five most frequently portrayed occupations on American television according to race and sex*

Males Occupation	%	Females Occupation	%
		Blacks	
(N = 95)		(N = 20)	
Govt diplomat	18.9	Nurse	30.0
Musician	13.7	Stage/Dancer	15.0
Policeman	9.5	Musician	5.0
Guard	9.5	Govt diplomat	5.0
Serviceman	5.3	Lawyer	5.0
Total	56.9	Secretary	5.0
		Total	65.0
		British	
(N = 104)		(N = 17)	
Guard	13.5	Nurse	41.2
Musician	11.5	Secretary	11.8
Waiter	7.7	Maid	5.9
Physician	4.8	Govt diplomat	5.9
Serviceman	4.8	Actress	5.9
Total	42.3	Total	70.7
		White Americans	
(N = 1,112)		(N = 260)	
Physician	7.6	Secretary	15.4
Policeman	7.6	Nurse	15.0
Musician	4.8	Stage/Dancer	8.1
Serviceman	4.6	Maid	6.5
Govt diplomat	4.5	Model	5.0
Total	29.1	Total	50.0

Note
N = actual numbers in sample

thirty seconds, and that each shot was more likely to show active movement. They concluded that even the style of commercials was helping to socialize boys into taking a more active attitude and girls into a more passive, static one.

What these examples show is that much of the interest of content analysis derives from the choice of unit to be counted, and that this count should involve a comparison.

If I have concentrated on the content analysis of gender portrayal, it is only for an example. The range of units that can be counted is almost infinite. For instance, Dallas Smythe (1953) found that television drama under-represented the very old (those over 60) and the young (those under

Table 4 *Occupations of males and females in television advertisements*

Female (N = 230)	%	Male (N = 155)	%
Housewife/mother	56	Husband/father	14
Stewardess	8	Professional athlete	12
Model	7	Celebrity	8
Celebrity/singer/dancer	5	Construction worker	7
Cook/maid/servant	3	Salesman	6
Secretary/clerical	3	Businessman	6
		Pilot	6
		Criminal	5
		Mechanic	3
		Lawyer	3
		Radio/TV interviewer	3
Other jobs scoring less than five per cent	18	Other jobs scoring less than five per cent	27

20). He found that white-collar jobs were heavily over-represented and working-class jobs were consequently under-represented. De Fleur's work (1964) supported this finding. Sidney Head (1954) found that 68 per cent of the television drama population was male, and that only 15 per cent was of lower class. He compared crime in the world of television with crime in society and found that murder constitutes 14 per cent of crime in the television world, but only 0.65 per cent of crime in the real world. Rape is more common than murder in real life, but it never occurred at all in the world of television. Gerbner (1970) also found a difference between real-life crime and television crime: for instance, television violence is usually between strangers for gain, power, or duty, whereas real-life violence is usually between intimates out of anger, frustration, or revenge.

Strikes and the media

The Glasgow Media Group (1976, 1980) have analysed the television coverage of industrial news. One of their many interesting findings was the disproportionately high coverage given to strikes in the motor industry, transport, and public administration, and the correspondingly low coverage of strikes in engineering (see table 5).

Before commenting on these figures, we must investigate one simple and obvious cause. Was this pattern of reporting simply a reflection of a pattern in reality; in other words, were there actually more strikes in these industries than in others? Table 6 shows that this was not the case.

Table 5 *Major areas of industrial dispute coverage on television, expressed as a percentage of total dispute coverage (January–May 1975)*

Industry category	Total % reports
Motor vehicles	28.0
Transport	27.0
Public administration	22.2
Total	77.2
Engineering	5.3
n = 805	

The table gives figures for principal disputes only. The Glasgow Media Group find that figures for all stoppages, the total number of working days lost, and the total number of workers involved all revealed the same disproportionate concentration on three industries.

Table 6 *Principal disputes compared to television reports*

Industry	No. of stoppages recorded by Dept of Employment	No. of strikes reported by TV bulletins
Engineering	6	1
Shipbuilding	1	–
Motor vehicles	7	5
Other manufacturing	1	–
Transport and communication	2	2
Miscellaneous	1	1
Public administration	2	2
Total	20	11

Table 7 takes a different approach. This compares the Department of Employment statistics with the Press Association reports (that is, what was available for publication/broadcasting) with what was published in the press and on television.

Content analysis reveals that the media distortion is there, and that television's coverage is more disproportionate than that of the press, even though the rank orders of the two media are the same. What content analysis cannot do is to help us answer the question, why? It does not presume to tell us if this pattern reflects the intimate love–hate relationship of the British public with cars and with its local authorities, or if it reflects the media editors' belief in this relationship, or if it merely

Table 7 *Press and television coverage of particular economic sectors*

Sector	Dept of Employment Working days lost		Dept of Employment Workers involved		Press Association Dispute items		Press Dispute items		TV Dispute items	
	Rank	%	Rank	%	Rank	%	Rank	%	Rank	%
January										
Vehicles	3	10.1	2	18.76	2	27	1	33.4	1	41.5
Transport	5	7.8	1	24.7	3	11	3	21.5	3	7.5
Public admin.	6	6.5	7	3.0	1	29	2	17	2	24.1
February										
Vehicles	1	18.4	1	23.1	3	17.3	3	16.4	2	19.3
Public admin.	3	15.1	7	5.7	2	37.3	2	17.6	3	13.4
Transport	5	7.0	3	11.5	1	4.0	1	51	1	60.5

reflects an unquestioning adherence to journalistic tradition that certain areas are 'news' and others are not.

Football on television

Drama, news, current affairs are all composed of obviously countable units. Football on television may seem less amenable to this method, but Charles Barr (1975) produced some interesting results when comparing the style of the West German presentation of the 1974 World Cup with that of the BBC's *Match of the Day*. What he chose to count was how frequently a close shot was inserted into the basic wider shot of about one-eighth of the pitch. The average time it took to register fifty shots was:

West German television   12 minutes 45 seconds
BBC *Match of the Day*   6 minutes 57 seconds

The difference may have been caused by the fact that *Match of the Day* is an edited recording of highlights, and that highlights are naturally shot in close-up. This hypothesis assumes that quieter periods of midfield play are shown in long shot, whereas goal-mouth drama, free kicks, arguments, corners, and so on are shown in close-up. To test this, Barr did a content analysis of what was shown in close-up. He studied twenty-five close-ups from each of three West German television matches and from two editions of *Match of the Day*, to find out if close-ups were used when the ball was in or out of play. His results averaged out as in table 8.

Table 8   *Use of close-ups in television football coverage*

	Close-ups used when:	
	ball in play	ball out of play
West German television	7	18 ⎱ per 25
BBC 'Match of the Day'	16.5	8.5 ⎰ close-ups

Closer analysis showed that the difference was even more marked. In one West German television match, out of nine consecutive close-ups showing the ball in play, only one showed a player running with the ball in an open situation, five showed the goalkeeper with the ball, one showed a player whose shot had been saved, one a player shielding the ball as it ran out of play, and the last a player about to be fouled.

Conversely, the majority of the British television's close-ups showed players running with the ball in an open situation.

The trouble with much content analysis is that it tends to leave one asking 'so what?' Are the differences here significant, and if so in what way? Is the audience different? Perhaps the British audience is less specialist and needs its football made more dramatic by the use of editing and camera work. Barr quotes Alec Weekes, producer of *Match of the Day*, saying, 'What about the development of action replay and other specialist shots? They are for the mums and daughters really. The fan would be quite content to see a one-camera coverage.' Close-ups concentrate on the stars, on the personal skills, on dramatic conflicts between individuals. Long shots show team work, the less dramatic but skilful running off the ball, the more specialist tactical positioning. Are the high transfer fees, the press and television attention given to great players or personalities, and the television style of presenting football all signs that we see football as another branch of showbiz with a star system as its core? Does Germany see its football as a more tactical team game? Content analysis can never answer speculative, large-scale questions like this, but at least it can provide us with some data upon which to base our discussion.

Gerbner, content, and culture

The worker who has produced the most fully developed theory of how content analysis can shed light on deeper cultural matters like this is George Gerbner. He believes that a culture communicates with itself through its total mass-media output, and that this communication maintains or modifies the broad consensus of values in a culture. For him, the great strength of content analysis is that it analyses the whole message system, and not the individual's selective experience of it. It is the 'massness', that which is available to the culture as a whole, that is significant, and it is this with which content analysis can cope. Gerbner thinks that the important characteristics of the media are the patterns that lie under the whole output, not the individual television programme. These patterns are absorbed gradually by the viewers, without their ever becoming consciously aware of them. Gerbner's analysis is aimed at revealing these patterns. Much of his work has been on the portrayal of violence on television.

Killers: Killed The amount of violence has been well documented. Gerbner (1970) shows that eight out of ten plays on American television contained violence; five out of ten leading characters committed it; six out of ten suffered it. There were four hundred casualties per week. But the significant patterns start to emerge when he analyses who are the violents and who are the victims: one pattern is revealed by his killers:killed ratio. Killing is the most extreme and efficient form of violence and is critical in distinguishing heroes from villains; and identifying the types of people who kill and the types who are killed can tell us much about the social values in a particular society. It is, for instance, comparatively rare for a white, middle-class male in his prime of life (say aged 18–30) to be killed, but he is a comparatively common killer. Gerbner sees this as a direct reflection of social values: we rate highly the middle class, whiteness, and youth. His full figures are given in table 9. On figures like these Gerbner bases his conclusion that violence on television is a dramatic portrayal of power and influence in society. The social groups who are most valued are most likely to provide the heroes who are, in turn, most likely to be the successful violents. Conversely, the least-valued social groups are most likely to provide the victims. Content analysis is the only method which can reveal such large-scale patterns in television output as a whole.

Table 9   *The ratios of killers to killed on American television in terms of age, class, and race*

	Killers		Killed
Age			
Young adult	5	:	1
Middle-aged	2	:	1
Old	1	:	1
Class			
Upper	1	:	1
Middle	3	:	1
Lower	1	:	1
Race			
White American	4	:	1
White foreigner	3	:	2
Non-white	1	:	1

Content analysis and cultural values

While content analysis concerns itself with the denotative order of communication, it can, and does, reveal patterns and frequencies within this order that connote values and attitudes. The early content analysts confined their conclusions to this denotative order and thus missed many of the more interesting, though perhaps more speculative, conclusions of workers like Gerbner, Dominick and Rauch, or Seggar and Wheeler. We can deduce some general laws relating content analysis in the denotative order to connotations of social values: the over-representation of men, white-collar jobs, and certain age-groups and races leads to the conclusion that frequency of portrayal connotes a high rank in the value system. Or that a character's position in the structure of violent relationships connotes the relative centrality or deviance of his or her social group in real life. Being a victim on television is a metaphor for being of low status in real life. (Remember how there are similarities in the workings of connotation and metaphor.)

Semantic differential

Meaning, we have argued, is a dynamic interaction between reader and message. A reader is constituted by her or his socio-cultural experience and is thus the channel through which message and culture interact. This is meaning. So content analysis, with its exclusive focus upon the whole message system, can provide data relevant to only part of this interaction that we call meaning. We need to study the reader as well.

One common method of doing this is known as the *semantic differential*. It was developed by Charles Osgood (1967) as a way of studying people's feelings, attitudes, or emotions towards certain concepts. If we assume that these feelings, attitudes, and emotions are derived largely from the individual's socio-cultural experience, then we find that Osgood is trying to measure what Barthes calls 'connotations'. The method is simple; it involves three stages:

1. Identifying the values to be investigated and expressing these as binarily opposed concepts on a five- or seven-point scale. Usually eight to fifteen values will be sufficient.
2. Asking a sample, or selected groups, to record their reactions on each scale.
3. Averaging the results.

Meaning of camera angle

An illustration is the best way to explain it. Baggaley and Duck (1976) decided that they wanted to test if there was a difference in meaning between a television presenter addressing the camera directly and in three-quarter profile. They made two simultaneous video recordings of a presenter, one from a camera that he was addressing, and one from a camera shooting him in three-quarter shot from the same distance. The only difference between the two video recordings was the camera angle.

Stage 1, they generated fourteen values to test (see figure 24). The correct way to generate the values is to show the video tapes to a pilot sample and to ask the audience to discuss freely their subjective responses to the tapes. This discussion can be prompted to go in certain directions, but the experimenter should be careful not to interfere or introduce bias. The discussion is recorded and then analysed to find the most commonly used adjectives or expressions of value. These form the basis of the value scales to be used. Stage 2, Baggaley and Duck showed each video tape to a different but similar audience and asked them to record their responses on the scales. Neither audience knew of the existence of the other tape or audience, nor what was the significant aspect of the tape they were watching. Stage 3, the mean ratings were worked out and presented as figure 24.

The audiences were small (only twelve), so we can only count large differences as significant. Thus shooting the presenter in three-quarter shot connotes considerably greater expertise, reliability, and sincerity and makes him appear more humane, fair, precise, tolerant, emotional, and relaxed. This is an interesting result, particularly when we consider how many television presenters, and politicians, like to address the camera

	1	2	3	4	5	6	7	
Ruthless				+----o				Humane
Fair		o----+						Unfair
Imprecise			+----o					Precise
Expert			o------+					Inexpert
Partial	+o							Impartial
Weak				+o				Forceful
Intolerant			+---o					Tolerant
Cautious				+o				Rash
Unemotional			+----o					Emotional
Intuitive			+o					Rational
Relaxed		o----+						Unrelaxed
Direct		o---+						Evasive
Unreliable			+----o					Reliable
Sincere		o--------+						Insincere

Figure 24   *Mean ratings of a television presenter seen (+) addressing camera and (o) in three-quarter profile*

directly. What Baggaley and Duck have done is to provide an empirical version of the commutation test (see p. 109). They have actually, not imaginatively, changed a unit in a syntagm and have actually, not imaginatively, tested the difference in meaning that it made.

Their work also enables us to make some interesting further points about codes and conventions. They show that a presenter in three-quarter shot appears more sincere, more direct, more expert, and generally presents a better set of connoted values. This may be surprising, for in real-life codes, facing the listener squarely is usually taken to indicate sincerity, directness, expertise, and so on. This points to an interesting distinction between real-life codes and television codes, and it is a distinction that needs stressing because television's apparent similarity to real life can all too easily lead us to the fallacious belief that television codes and real-life codes are the same. They are not: we do not respond to a televised event in the same way as to a live event.

In this case the television code has developed through convention and usage. People televised addressing the camera are nearly always media professionals who perform a script, that is who speak other people's words. But people televised in three-quarter shot are usually the experts being interviewed, the eyewitnesses who saw what actually happened. They are the honest experts speaking their own words. And they are speaking to an interviewer or reporter, not to the camera: we note how it jars if they do turn and address the camera directly.

This is a clear example of how television convention differs from real-life convention and how this difference has produced different codes. These codes are codes of connotation; they derive from the form of the signifier (which is altered by the change of camera angle). The denoted meaning is the same for each video tape. It should be possible, using the semantic differential, to construct the paradigm of significantly different camera angles. Possibly there are four: full face, three-quarter shot, profile, and from the rear. But if these differences are significant, they can have gained this significance only through convention and usage producing this unspoken agreement amongst the users.

The view in the mirror

Another example of the way that the semantic differential can be used to check theoretical readings with empirical data is provided by an investigation carried out by one of my students, Jennifer Farish. She wanted to test the predictions made in chapter 1 (p. 16) about the different readings of plates 1a and 1b. She showed plate 1a to twenty-five subjects, and plate 1b to a different twenty-five. She asked each subject to record his or her reaction on the semantic differential scales shown in figure 25. She also checked each subject's attitude to the police before showing the picture, and found that there was no significant difference in attitudes towards the police between those who saw plate 1a and those who saw plate 1b. The results of her survey are summarized in figure 25.

Please indicate your reactions to the police behaviour shown here. (NB '4' is always neutral. The more you mark to the left of '4', the more strongly you agree with the value on the left: the more you mark to the right of '4', the more strongly you agree with the value on the right.)

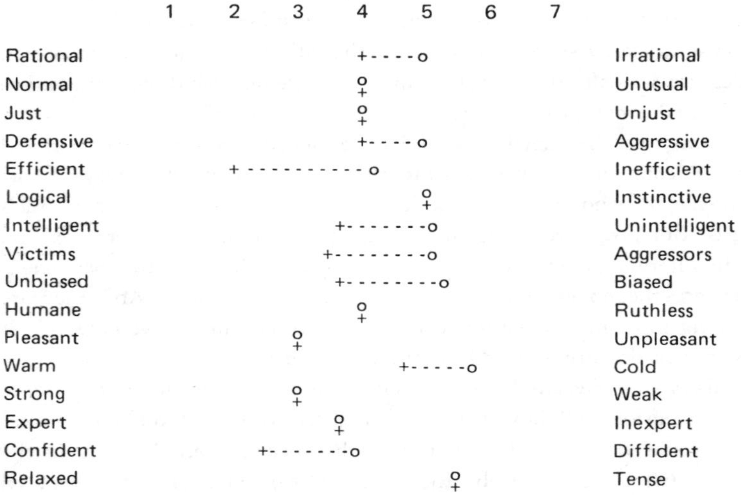

```
              1     2     3     4     5     6     7

Rational                        + - - - - o                    Irrational
Normal                          o                              Unusual
                                +
Just                            o                              Unjust
                                +
Defensive                       + - - - - o                    Aggressive
Efficient           + - - - - - - - - - - o                    Inefficient
Logical                               o                        Instinctive
                                      +
Intelligent               + - - - - - - - o                    Unintelligent
Victims                 + - - - - - - - o                      Aggressors
Unbiased                  + - - - - - - - - o                  Biased
Humane                          o                              Ruthless
                                +
Pleasant            o                                          Unpleasant
                    +
Warm                                        + - - - - - o      Cold
Strong              o                                          Weak
                    +
Expert                    o                                    Inexpert
                          +
Confident           + - - - - - - o                            Diffident
Relaxed                               o                        Tense
                                      +
```

Figure 25   *Averaged reactions of those who saw the full page, plate 1b (+), and of those who saw only the photograph in plate 1a (O)*

As usual, the semantic differential produced some surprises, though overall the results are very much what we would predict. The average reaction to the full page (plate 1b) is more to the left (where the more favourable and common values are) than the reaction to the main photograph on its own. The full page made the police appear markedly more efficient and more confident. As we predicted, it also made them appear less biased (though this difference does not show up on the Just/Unjust scale); similarly, they appeared more rational and more intelligent and, interestingly, less cold.

What the averaging technique fails to show, however, is how the average was arrived at. For instance, the responses to the Logical/Instinctive and the Relaxed/Tense scales showed a high degree of agreement, whereas the average score on the Just/Unjust and the Pleasant/Unpleasant scales concealed a wide range of differing reactions. We would need further work to account for these different patterns of response: for instance, we would need to find out *who* reacted with a 1 or a 7 on the Just/Unjust scale. It may be that factors like social class, race, sex, or political persuasion were crucial in determining people's responses.

We would also need to investigate a possible explanation for the fact that some scales produced a wide variation of response while others produced a more homogeneous one. It may be that the widely varied responses occur on scales where the audience already hold strong views: the 'readings' are as varied as the audience members, and the text has comparatively little influence upon them. Conversely, the homogeneous responses may well occur where the audience's views are less strongly held, and consequently the text is able to exert a greater influence upon the response. The negotiation between text and reader produces a meaning that in the first case is determined more by the reader and in the second by the text.

But what the investigation has provided is evidence for the view that the context of the full front page has made the original photograph fit better with the conventional picture of the police: it has made it activate the dominant *myth* more easily; it has made it more *redundant*, and thus more typical of a mass medium. It may also make us wonder whether the *Daily Mirror* reflects reality or the audience.

Heroes, villains, and victims

Gerbner (1970) combines the semantic differential with his content analysis. Having identified the social groupings within the killers:killed relationship, he then went on to investigate how the audience saw the personalities of three categories of characters:

1. Killers, final outcome happy (these were the killers who won in the end, that is, the heroes).
2. Killers, final outcome unhappy (that is, the villains).
3. The killed (the victims).

His results are given in figure 26. These show that the only significant differences between heroes and villains were that heroes were more attractive and more efficient. This pattern of efficiency may well reflect the fact that we live in a competitive, Darwinian society, where the fittest survive and where efficiency is an inevitable correlate of success.

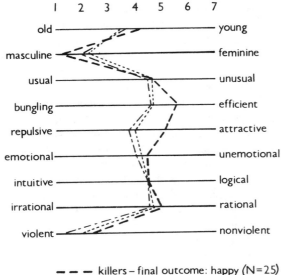

Figure 26   *Personality profiles of 'killers' and 'killed'*

Inefficiency is deviant in a competitive society and thus naturally correlates with villainy.

Cultivation

Gerbner has taken the empirical study of communication further than any other worker. This is because he uses the data derived from content analysis and audience study to form the basis of the theory of how the mass-media system relates to the culture from which it grows and to which it speaks. He calls this relationship one of 'cultivation'; that is, the media cultivate attitudes and values in a culture. They do not create them – they must already be there; but they nurture, propagate, and help the culture to maintain and adapt its values, to spread them among its members, and thus to bind these members with a shared consensus, an intersubjectivity. Content analysis reveals the values embedded in the total message system of a culture; the semantic differential can investigate whether these values are actually 'cultivated' in the reader.

Uses and gratifications theory

There are many empirical studies of the audience, particularly of the mass media. The bulk of this work has been on the effects of the portrayal of violence. Psychologists have conducted laboratory experiments, and sociologists have conducted large-scale field studies. Such work is outside the scope of this book. But I wish to introduce the reader to one other empirical method, that known as the *uses and gratifications* approach. This approach takes as its basis the belief that the audience has a complex set of needs which it seeks to satisfy in the mass media. There are, of course, other ways of satisfying needs – holidays, sport, hobbies, work, etc. It is a theory developed to explain mass communication, though it fits very well with theories of face-to-face communication which postulate that we use social relationships to satisfy personal needs and drives. This model of communication assumes an audience that is at least as active as the sender. It also implies that a message is what the audience makes of it, not what the sender intends, and thus has some similarity with the semiotic method.

Uses of quiz programmes

The usual method of the uses and gratifications approach is a questionnaire in which members of the television audience are asked to give their main reasons for watching a particular type of programme. An example of the sort of results that this approach can yield is provided by McQuail, Blumler, and Brown (1972). In their study of the audience of television, they found, amongst other things, that there were groups of broadly similar 'uses' that people made of television quiz programmes. Table 10 summarizes their findings. Most of the audience used quiz programmes for four main gratifications: self-rating, social interaction, excitement, and education. Investigating further, McQuail and his colleagues discovered that most of those who 'used' quiz programmes for self-rating gratifications lived in council houses and were members of the working class. We might speculate that they were using the media to give themselves a personal status which their social life did not. This is a clear example of the *compensatory* use of the media to gratify needs that the rest of social life frustrates. Those who tended to use the programmes as a basis for social interaction were, not surprisingly, highly sociable types who reported a large number of acquaintances in their neighbourhoods. They used the media to provide subjects of conversation. The media here are *supplementing* other sources of need gratification. The excitement appeal was reported most often by working-class viewers who were not very sociable. Again, a compensatory motive would seem to operate here. The educational appeal was clearly compensatory, in that those who reported this as the major gratification were ones who had left school at the minimum age.

Uses of crime series

A student of mine, Simon Morris, made a uses and gratification study of people's use of television crime series. He found, again, a variety of uses of the programmes: viewers used them for excitement, escapism; many for information – 'they give us a picture of what life is like in big cities'; and many for reassurance – 'I like seeing law and order triumph in the end', or 'they make me feel glad I'm living safely in our little town'. A critical factor he found was not class or education, but age. The 18–30 age-group stressed the excitement/escapism gratification, whereas those aged over 50 tended to find information and reassurance in the programme.

Categories of gratification

Though different workers label and categorize the gratifications differently, there is none the less a remarkable measure of agreement amongst them. McQuail's four main categories (outlined below) are typical, and few other workers would disagree with them fundamentally.

1. *Diversion*
(a) Escape from the constraints of routine;
(b) Escape from the burdens of problems;
(c) Emotional release.
All studies reveal similar escapist needs in the media audience. McQuail does at least hint that we need to go further than merely labelling these needs escapist – we need to identify what we are escaping from. Semiotic analyses of the programmes can also show us what we are escaping *to*.

2. *Personal relationships*
(a) Companionship;
(b) Social utility.
'Companionship' is the media as compensation in a particularly clear form. Housewives have the radio on because they like the sound of voices in the house in the daytime. Lonely people who may find it difficult to make real social relationships turn to the media for friendship. They

Table 10   *Gratifications of television quiz programmes*

Cluster 1   Self-rating appeal

I can compare myself with the experts

I like to imagine that I am on the programme and doing well

I feel pleased that the side I favour has actually won

I imagine that I was on the programme and doing well

I am reminded of when I was in school

I laugh at the contestant's mistakes

Hard to follow

Cluster 2   Basis for social interaction

I look forward to talking about it with others

I like competing with other people watching with me

I like working together with the family on the answers

I hope the children will get a lot out of it

The children get a lot out of it

It brings the family together sharing the same interest

It is a topic of conversation afterwards

Not really for people like myself

Cluster 3   Excitement appeal

I like the excitement of a close finish

I like to forget my worries for a while

I like trying to guess the winner

Having got the answer right I feel really good

I completely forget my worries

I get involved in the competition

Exciting

Cluster 4   Educational appeal

I find I know more than I thought

I feel I have improved myself

I feel respect for the people on the programme

I think over some of the questions afterwards

Educational

Cluster 5

It is nice to see the experts taken down a peg

It is amusing to see the mistakes some of the contestants make

Cluster 6

I like to learn something as well as to be entertained

I like finding out new things

Cluster 7

I like trying to guess the answers

I hope to find that I know some of the answers

Cluster 8

I find out the gaps in what I know

I learn something new

A waste of time

Subjects were given a questionnaire with these statements in random order. They were asked to indicate which statements reflected the gratifications they found in quiz programmes. Their answers tended to 'cluster' — that is, it was found that a subject who answered positively to one statement in a cluster was statistically likely to answer positively to most of the rest.

believe in the characters of *Coronation Street* and *Crossroads* and send them birthday cards because they *need* to. Their social or personal situation does not allow them to satisfy their need for companionship in real life. The 'social utility' use is usually the provision of something to talk about. The media provide a shared experience, a shared topic of conversation that makes social interaction that much easier. If all your friends saw a programme and you did not, you feel temporarily excluded from their group.

3. *Personal identity*
(a) Personal reference;
(b) Reality exploration;
(c) Value reinforcement.

By 'personal reference' McQuail refers to the way viewers use a programme as a point of direct comparison with their real life: 'I can compare the people in the programme with other people I know', or 'it reminds me of things that have happened in my life', are typical uses that he quotes. 'Reality exploration' involves a direct use of the programme content to help the viewer understand their own life. Typical quotations are: 'The people in the Dales have problems that are like my own'; 'It sometimes helps me to understand my own life'. 'Value reinforcement' is self-explanatory: 'it puts over a picture of what family life should be like' or 'it reminds me of the importance of family ties'.

4. *Surveillance* This is the need for information about the complex world we live in. Other studies have shown that people whom we can call 'opinion leaders' in their social life use the media for information in order to maintain their social role.

Social origin of needs

Blumler and Katz (1974) stress the social origin of the needs that the media gratify. Their findings are summarized in table 11.

Bases of uses and gratifications studies

The assumptions upon which this approach is based, then, can be outlined as follows:

1. The audience is active. It is not a passive receiver of whatever the media broadcast. It selects and uses progamme content.

Table 11 *Social origin of audience needs and the media*

Social origin of audience needs	Media provide
The social situation:	
(a) Produces tension and conflict	Easement
(b) Creates awareness of problems that demand attention	Information
(c) Impoverishes opportunities to satisfy certain needs	Complementary, substitute, or supplementary servicing
(d) Gives rise to certain values	Affirmation and reinforcement
(e) Provides expectations of familiarity with certain media materials	Shared experience to sustain membership of valued social groupings

2. Audience members freely select the media and the programmes that they can best use to gratify their needs. The media producer may not be aware of the uses to which the programme may be put, and different audience members may use the same programme to gratify different needs.

3. The media are not the only source of gratification. Going on holiday, playing sport, dancing, etc. are all used as the media are used.

4. People are, or can be made, aware of their interests and motives in particular cases. (For critics of this method, this is the assumption that is weakest. Such critics argue that the motives that can be articulated are often the least important, and that to link audience and programme content only by a rational chain of needs and gratifications is limiting 'meaning' unacceptably.)

5. Value judgements about the cultural significance of the mass media must be suspended. It is irrelevant to say that *Crossroads* is trash: if it meets the needs of seven million people it is *useful*, and the fact that it offends highbrow aesthetes is neither here nor there.

Method

A simple uses and gratifications questionnaire can be compiled in much the same way as a semantic differential. The investigator should record unstructured discussions with a sample audience in order to generate a number of stated motives for watching. These are then printed in random order on the questionnaire, and the respondents invited to record the strength of their agreement or disagreement with each motive. Morris's questionnaire looked like figure 27.

This is part of a study of reasons for enjoying detective/crime series on television. Will you please indicate how strongly you agree or disagree with each of the following statements, by placing a tick in the appropriate column. (1 = strongly agree, 2 = agree, 3 = neutral, 4 = disagree, 5 = strongly disagree.)

Reason for watching	1	2	3	4	5
I like to identify with the hero					
I like to talk about the shows with others					
I like the tension of not knowing what is going to happen					
It makes me aware of how difficult a job the police have					
I like to imagine how I would cope with a violent situation					
Etc.					

Note
It is usually necessary to collect some data about the respondent: sex, age, occupation, educational level.

Figure 27   *Uses and gratifications questionnaire*

Identifying the significant patterns in the results is the hardest part of the operation. Academic researchers use a statistical technique known as cluster analysis which would be inappropriate for most readers of this book. Less pure, but more practical, is to identify the 'appeal clusters' of the statements before devising the questionnaire. It is then fairly simple to compare, say, male with female responses to statements in the 'excitement/diversion' cluster. Basic significant correlations or patterns can be revealed without sophisticated statistical method, though more advanced analysis will require correspondingly advanced analytical techniques.

Audience ethnographies

Empirical methods tend to treat communication as a series of messages whose content is the equivalent of factual data: they have no theory of texts of signification, and thus take no account of the processes of decoding or reading. Semiotics and structuralism are concerned with the way that communication structures (and therefore generates) meaning in order to circulate it socially. They trace the interconnections between the structure of communication messages and the structure of the society in which they work. For them, messages do not contain or convey meaning, but are agents in its production and circulation. They are therefore agents of social power.

Structuralism and semiotics can be criticized, however, for moving too easily between textual and social structures, and for ignoring the fact that, in practice, the connections between text and society can be made only through the addressee or reader. It is in the act or process of reading that text and society meet. Ethnographic study has developed in order to investigate this process and to test semiotic or structuralist readings of texts by comparing them to the readings that people actually make, or say they make.

In general, the findings suggest that semiotics and structuralism overestimate the power of the text to promote a dominant or preferred reading and underestimate the ability of readers to make sense of the text in ways that relate it directly to their social situation. So a semiotic analysis of popular romance novels, such as those published by Mills and Boon or Harlequin, could well conclude that their social function is to train women for a submissive role in marriage, to centre their happiness upon the love of a strong man, and to teach that their suffering, which the cruel side of his strength will make them undergo, will finally be rewarded because in it he will see their true worth. It is, of course, easy to relate this textual structure with the social structuring of gender roles in a patriarchal society. But Radway (1984), for instance, found that some women readers did not read the novels in this way. They preferred novels with a spirited, rebellious heroine, who kicked against her victimization by the hero. For them the plot did not trace the victimization and suffering of the heroine through which she achieved final success (marriage), but instead traced the gradual feminization of the hero: only when his cruelty had been softened, his cold aloofness warmed up, and he had become more sensitive towards her, only when he had been 'feminized' in this way would she consent to marry him. While the structure of the novels preferred masculine values over feminine ones, some readers 'negotiated' the text to produce readings that validated feminine values over masculine.

For some women, the social context of reading was at least as important as the text: their social situation was one of unrelenting service to the demands of their husband and family: by reading a novel they were able to create a time and a space of their own in which they could put themselves first (often in defiance of the explicit disapproval of their husbands). One 'meaning' of reading romance was the assertion of their own rights and self-worth – a meaning that could not be analysed in the text, for it was produced at the moment of reading when the text met the social situation of the reader. One woman even reported that reading romances in this way gave her the self-confidence to stand up to the demands of her husband and demand more equality in their marriage.

Morley (1986) found similar significance in the way that television was watched in the family. In the urban lower-class families he studied, watching television was also part of the gender politics of the family but, unlike romance-reading, it promoted male power. The remote-control device typically lived on the arm of the husband's chair; his power was exerted in three domains – what to watch, how to watch it, and how to evaluate it.

The family viewing was organized around male tastes. Men's tastes were for factual programmes – news, sport, documentaries; or, if they watched fiction, they liked it to be 'realistic', which meant that they had to be able to recognize the outside world with which they were familiar in the programme. They also liked action drama. Women's tastes, on the other hand, were for 'family' dramas, soap operas, and romances, where the emphasis was on relationships rather than action, and whose knowledge was that of the interior world of emotions and reactions, not the exterior world of men.

Not only did men dominate what was watched; they also tried to control *how* it was watched. For the man, the house is a place of leisure where he can relax and indulge himself after work, so he likes to give himself up entirely to television and watch concentratedly. For the woman, however, the home is a place of work, and she has to fit television-watching in with her domestic labour – which includes not only washing, ironing, sewing, and other forms of housework, but also talking to the children, for the woman's role includes managing the relationships and human resources of the house as well as its material ones. So women watched television distractedly, almost always doing something else at the same time. This often annoyed the men, who frequently complained of the noise and chatter of the women and children while they were watching their programmes.

Women often used VCRs to timeshift their programmes to outside their working day, whose limits seemed to be set by the presence of other family members. They would record their programmes and watch them with full attention either early in the morning or late at night when everyone else was in bed, or sometimes they would find a 'window' in the early afternoon when the morning's work was done and the children had not yet returned from school.

These different ways of watching were, of course, determined socially, that is by the organization of work; they are not innate characteristics of the male and female sexes. So women who worked outside the home tended to watch television in similar ways to the men who did. Gender relationships are political because they are determined by social forces, not by nature.

This masculine domination extended even to the evaluation of the programmes. So masculine tastes were labelled as serious, good television, whereas the programmes that women liked were called trivial, light, or trashy. Soap opera (which appeals largely to women) is commonly considered the lowest form of television, and, in literature, romances are equally often used to typify the lowest form of the novel. The relationship between critical evaluation and social position is not, of course, coincidental, for devaluing women's cultural tastes is another way of subordinating them socially. An important point to make here is that women typically internalize masculine values and will often disparage their own cultural tastes (and thus, implicitly, themselves) by calling them 'trashy stuff' or 'silly'. This is an example of women participating in the ideology that subordinates them, an issue that we will explore in more detail in the next chapter when we discuss theories of ideology.

The ways in which texts are used socially may not be apparent in the structure of the texts themselves and thus may not be available for textual analysis. Equally, some of the meanings of texts may not be revealed by a textual analysis because they are produced at the moment when the text meets the social situation of the reader, and in this meeting the reader may bring unanticipated, non-textual factors to the process of making meaning.

So Hodge and Tripp (1986) found that Australian school students read a television soap opera called *Prisoner* in a particular way. The show was set in a women's prison and centred on the relationships that the prisoners and wardens formed amongst and between themselves. The school students made meanings of the programme that were relevant to their experience of school. They read the prison as a kind of metaphor for the school. Both were institutions designed to turn their inmates into the sort of people society wanted them to be, rather than what they themselves wanted to be; in both there was the sense that real life went on outside. Both attempted to control every aspect of their inmates' lives, and in both there were areas where this control was resisted – the toilets and bicycle sheds in schools, the laundry in the prison. There were similar types amongst both wardens and teachers – the bully, the soft new one, the decent one, and so on. Prisoners and students used similar ways of communicating under the eyes of wardens/teachers by winks and secret notes. The similarities were numerous.

There was nothing in the text that explicitly referred to school. These meanings were made as the text was brought into contact with the social situation of its viewers. They were not available to semiotic or structural analysis, but could be discovered only by ethnography. There is also some evidence that these socially relevant meanings became part of the school students' behaviour, for many teachers wrote to the programme producers complaining that it taught indiscipline and made their jobs harder. While semiotic and structuralist theory can allow for different readings being produced from the same text, and Hall and Eco both argue that this must happen with the mass media, ethnography can give us insight into some of the readings that are produced in specific situations, and can thus put some flesh on the bones of the theory.

I investigated the different readings of a particular moment in the television show *The NewlyWed Game* (Fiske 1989a). The four wives were off-camera when their husbands were asked 'Which would you say best sums up your wife's response recently to your "romantic needs"? "Yes, master", "No way, José", or "Get serious, man"?' All four men said that 'Yes, master' was the appropriate response; but when the wives came back on camera, two of them answered 'Yes, master', one 'Get serious, man' and the other 'No way, José'.

Different people read this small moment of popular culture in different ways. Some women, particularly those sympathetic to feminism, found the sexism in the question so powerfully offensive that for them the exchange was an example of patriarchy at its most blatant, particularly in its assumption that women's sexual pleasure could be defined only as a response to men's 'romantic needs'. Other women, however, found great pleasure and significance in the responses of those who refused to say 'Yes, master'. They were concerned more with how women coped with and struggled against patriarchal domination than with the domination itself. In the bits of experience that failed to fit into the dominant myth of marriage they found pro-feminine meanings that resisted and opposed the myth and its work in gender politics.

Some men produced 'dominant' readings: they laughed *with* the 'masterful' men on the show and laughed *at* the two with the less compliant wives. Other men, however, felt that the exchange, far from promoting patriarchy, actually exposed and interrogated it. They felt that the question put men on the spot, and that they would feel forced to answer 'Yes, master' in public, however much that might differ from their attitude in private with their wives. They felt that the embarrassment of the men whose wives 'showed them up' was greater than the embarrassment of the women who answered 'Yes, master'. They felt, in sum, that masculinity (as it is defined by patriarchy) came off far worse than femininity.

While all these readings 'read', in some way, the patriarchal structure of the text and the dominant myths of marriage and gender relations, they also produced meanings that differed from the dominant and in some cases contradicted it. The differences came from the different social situations of the readers, their gender, and the ways in which they lived their own gender relationships in their everyday lives. Their readings were not 'free' of the dominant, preferred one, but neither were they bound by it. Rather they were produced in co-operation with it, in reaction to it, or in counteraction against it. They provided some examples of how Hall's 'preferred reading' theory or Eco's one of 'aberrant decoding' could be seen in practice.

Ethnographic work can be both rewarding and full of problems. The rewards are its ability to see communication as a social as well as a textual practice, and to trace this social dimension not in large-scale socio-political theory but in the concrete circumstances of everyday life. Doing it involves observing people in the communication process and getting them to talk about their role in it as fully and openly as possible. But there are two types of problem involved here.

One is the role of the investigator, and the effect that his or her presence has. Traditionally, the ethnographer was taught to be objective and distant, to be a scientific observer in the empiricist mode. More recently, however, ethnographers have used their own experience as fans of the text in question to participate in the process rather than observe it. They join in discussion with the fans as equals, using their own experience as part of what they are studying, thus developing a rapport with their subjects that enables them to get a closer and more intimate insight into what the text means to them. Both Radway (1984) and Hobson (1982) have been particularly successful in this. The presence of the observer must make some difference – more sympathetic, friendly observers will inevitably get different responses from more distant, scientific ones; and this sort of ethnography cannot be an objective empirical science: it extends the interpretive analytical mode from texts to the people who read them and the meanings they make from them. It is thus an extension of semiotics and should perhaps be referred to by a name like 'ethno-semiotics'.

It has other problems which also differentiate it from empiricist work; these are the problems of interpreting the data it produces. It does not produce, as empiricism does, facts whose meanings are inherent in them, but further evidence of a cultural process at work that requires interpreting by a theoretically informed method just as does the original text.

The methodological model for ethno-semiotics, then, is linguistic, not empiricist. The audiences studied are not, as empiricism demands, representative of an objective social category, and the meanings they produce cannot be generalized out to that category as a whole. Ethnographic data is, rather, like a sentence to a linguist. As a sentence is an example of language in process, so ethnography can provide us with instances of communication in process. These instances or 'sentences' are typical of the process of communication and need to be understood within a theoretical framework, but they are not scientific facts. Recent theories of semiotics and structural linguistics teach us that meanings are always in process, always being made and remade, and are never completed facts. While it is always interesting and important to discover *which* meanings are made or preferred by texts and their socially situated readers, these meanings are never fixed and final, but are moments in the circulation of meaning within society; indeed, meanings exist only in their circulation.

Communication, then, is the study of meanings in their social circulation. Textual analysis is thus central to it. But the social dimension needs studying on two main levels – that of macro social structures, the distribution of power and resources within the social system in general, and that of the micro level where everyday life is lived and experienced. The socially conscious semiotics of Barthes and his theory of myth link textual structures with social structures. Ethno-semiotics links the reading of texts with the everyday lives of their readers.

The empirical methods outlined in this chapter should enable the reader to make some basic studies of the message and its audience. Comparing the results reached by semiotic analysis and empirical methods will raise important issues about the validity of each approach.

Suggestions for further work

1. Analyse the content of one evening's television advertisements in order to reveal both the pattern of occupational portrayal and the setting of men and women. Compare your findings with those of Dominick and Rauch in America in the early 1970s. What similarities and differences do you notice, and what is their significance? Make a semiotic analysis of selected advertisements. Does semiotics support or contradict content analysis?

Alternatively, do this exercise on magazines – women's or men's or teenager's, whichever type interests you most.

2. Use content analysis to compare a quality with a popular daily newspaper. Use the column centimetre as your unit. You should look at the ratio of editorial:advertising matter, of print:pictures, and of the space devoted to different categories of news topics. Hartley (1982), chapter 3, suggests the following topic categories: politics, the economy, foreign affairs, domestic news (divided into *hard news* – violence, conflict, crime – and *soft news* – warm-hearted and 'women's' stories), occasional stories (disasters, royalty, etc.), and sport. How adequate do you find these categories? Do you need any more – for example showbiz? What does this analysis tell you about the readership and communicative function of each paper? See also Dyer (1982), chapter 5.

3. Discover, by content analysis, the main themes and social attitudes of the lyrics of the top twenty pop songs.

4. Use the semantic differential to identify the main connotations of the type-faces you used in question 1 of chapter 5. You should use a sample of about twenty for each test. You may find the following pairs of adjectives useful: masculine–feminine, honest–dishonest, static–dynamic, cheap–expensive, serious–humorous, modern–old-fashioned, rural–urban, formal–informal, elegant–clumsy, authoritative–frivolous, accurate–inaccurate, important–unimportant, industrial–natural, upper-class–lower-class, aggressive–non-aggressive, secure–risky (generated by one of my students, Jenny Hughes).

5. Devise a 'uses and gratifications' questionnaire to investigate the uses the audience makes of a popular television or radio programme or programme type. Ones worth investigating include soap opera, *Tom and Jerry* (or other cartoons), crime series, quiz shows, record requests, national or local news – or any sort of programme that interests you. Or you can investigate types of pop music. Remember to relate your results to social position as defined by (for example) age, sex, occupation, family status, education. Do not feel you have to use all of these – your choice will depend on what you are investigating and on your audience. Compare your results to McQuail's categories of gratification. See Corner and Hawthorn (1980), pp. 187–201.

6. Conduct a small-scale ethnographic study of how your family or friends watch television. (See Fiske, 1987, chapter 5.)

9 IDEOLOGY AND MEANINGS

Signification and culture

In chapter 5 we were looking at the two orders of signification. This deliberately left some questions unasked, some topics unopened. The most important of these questions is how do these second-order meanings fit with the culture within which they operate? Where do the myths and connotations arise?

We have shown that their meanings are not located in the text itself. Reading is not akin to using a can opener to reveal the meaning in the message. Meanings are produced in the interactions between text and audience. Meaning production is a dynamic act in which both elements contribute equally. When the text and the audience are members of a tightly knit culture or subculture, the interaction is smooth and effortless: the connotations and myths upon which the text draws fit closely, if not exactly, with those of the audience members.

In other cases, the meanings are produced with a much greater sense of strain. The preferred reading of the Notting Hill photograph may come easily to some, but for others it may be the cause of stress or disagreement. They may decode it by oppositional or negotiated codes, not by the dominant 'easy' one. In other words, their myths by which they understand the police, the blacks, youth, urban living, and violence, to name the main ones, are different from those that the *Observer* assumes to be held by the majority of its readers. In fact semioticians would go further than this. They would argue that the *Observer* is not merely assuming that its readers share these second-order meanings, but actively making its reader into a 'white liberal democrat'. It is inviting the reader to assume this social identity in order to be able to decode the picture according to the dominant codes, or, to put it another way, to be able to arrive at the meanings that the picture itself prefers. The reader and the text together produce the preferred meaning, and in this collaboration the reader is constituted as someone with a particular set of relationships to the dominant value system and to the rest of society. This is ideology at work.

Ideology

There are a number of definitions of ideology. Different writers use the term differently, and it is not easy to be sure about its use in any one context. Raymond Williams (1977) finds three main uses:

1. A system of beliefs characteristic of a particular class or group.
2. A system of illusory beliefs — false ideas or false consciousness — which can be contrasted with true or scientific knowledge.
3. The general process of the production of meanings and ideas.

These are not necessarily contradictory, and any one use of the word may quite properly involve elements from the others. But they do, none the less, identify different foci of meanings. Let us take them consecutively.

Use 1 This is closer to the psychologists' use of the word. Psychologists use 'ideology' to refer to the way that attitudes are organized into a coherent pattern. Let us take, for example, a man who holds a particular set of attitudes about young people. He believes that a couple of years' National Service will give them all a 'bit of backbone' and solve most of our social problems. We may confidently predict the sort of attitudes that such a man will hold on subjects like crime and punishment, class, race, and religion. If our predictions are correct, we will be able to say that he has a right-wing, authoritarian ideology. It is this that gives shape and coherence to his attitudes and that enables him to fit them satisfactorily into each other. Or, as Brockreide (1968) succinctly puts it, 'attitudes have homes in ideologies'.

What few psychologists go on to argue, however, is that ideology is determined by society, not by the individual's possibly unique set of attitudes and experiences. Marxists, who tend to regard the term as their particular property, always relate ideology to social relations. It is socially determined, not individualistic. And for Marxists, the social fact that determines ideology is class, the division of labour.

Use 2   This leads us naturally on to Williams's second use of the term. Indeed, Williams suggests that in practice uses 1 and 2 will inevitably become conflated. Ideology, then, becomes the category of illusions and false consciousness by which the ruling class maintains its dominance over the working class. Because the ruling class controls the main means by which ideology is propagated and spread throughout society, it can then make the working class see its subordination as 'natural', and therefore right. Herein lies the falseness. These ideological media include the educational, political, and legal systems, and the mass media and publishing.

Such a reading of our Notting Hill photograph explains how the meanings of the photograph depend on the dominant ideology within which the photograph locates the reader. This ideology includes assumptions that the police are right, non-violent, defenders of our law and order, that they are *us*. The young blacks, on the other hand, are aggressive, anti-social, *them*. Taken on its own, as a unique, discrete text, this photograph might not necessarily seem to invite us to generate these meanings. But, of course, it cannot be taken on its own. It is part of our cultural experience: its reading is affected by readings of other photographs of police controlling demonstrators/riots. The meanings generated by any one text are determined partly by the meanings of other texts to which it appears similar. This is called 'intertextuality'. The reader of this book might well make a collection of portrayals of the police in these situations to see how the ideological force is clarified by the intertextuality of a number of photographs. Stuart Hall (1973b) gives a detailed and convincing analysis of a press photograph. It is of a policeman being kicked by a demonstrator during the anti-Vietnam War demonstrations in Grosvenor Square. Ideologically, his photograph and our photograph are identical.

Use 3   This is the most overarching of the three. Indeed, the three uses might almost be modelled as Chinese boxes – 1 is inside 2 which is inside 3. Ideology here is a term used to describe the social production of meanings. This is how Barthes uses it when he speaks of the connotators, that is the signifiers of connotation, as 'the rhetoric of ideology'. Ideology, used in this way, is the source of the second-order meanings. Myths and connoted values are what they are because of the ideology of which they are the usable manifestations.

Signs: ideology: meanings

An example will help us to clarify how ideology works to produce meaning through signs. Fiske (1979) has analysed a schools television programme transmitted by the BBC on 1 March 1979. It is called *Food and Population*, and its central point is, in the words of the commentary, 'We now know how to produce enough food to feed a continually growing population, yet many are starving because the scientific solutions are not being put into practice.' This point is made by a film of Peru which constrasts the primitive agriculture of an Andean village with the advances of science and technology in the cities and the developed coastal strip. But this point is also ideological: the statement is meaningful only in so far as its maker and audience are members of a science-based culture. This programme is structured around certain manifest oppositions:

> agricultural science : traditional farming
> market economy : subsistence economy
> city : country
> children as mouths to feed : children as hands to work
> progress : stasis, cyclical culture
> change : tradition

The deep binary opposition which structures the programme is, therefore, that between *science* and *non-science*. The deep structure of the programme, the ideological frame, may be expressed thus:

> *We* are to *them* as *science* is to *non-science*.

Plate 14 shows some of the manifestations of this structure in the programme. The programme is made by and for the culture on the left of the structure, the *we* and *science*, but it is primarily about those on the right, the *them* and *non-science*. In practice this is shown most clearly by devices like the way the commentary explains fully, if not a little patronizingly, the values and attributes of the non-science culture, while leaving those of the science culture assumed and taken for granted. This assumption that those values are so basic, so widely shared, so *natural* that they do not need referring to is what Barthes (1973) calls 'exnomination', and is ideology at work.

The ideology of science

The ideology of science is what this programme is really about. Take

City

Country

Children: mouths to feed

Children: hands to work

Women's work – city

Women's work – country

Plate 14   *Science:Non-science*

*Potatoes – specimens
in laboratory*

*Potatoes – crops drying
in the sun*

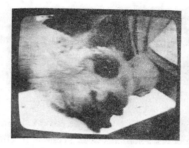

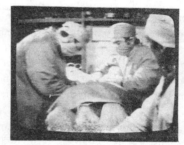

Alpaca on operating table

Alpaca on shearing table

plates 15a and 15b. They are different signifiers, but they have the same signified, the concept which we must already hold if we are to understand the signs of 'science'. There are obviously marginal differences in the signifiers, but the core of the signified is common to both signs. A member of the non-science culture to the right of our structure will inevitably have a different concept from ours. The signifier will be the same for both cultures, but the signified will differ significantly. And the difference in the signifieds is the difference in the ideologies.

Plate 15a *'Science'*   Plate 15b   *'Science'*

In the second order of signification, science is understood by a Barthesean myth which includes concepts such as, that science is the ultimate problem solver, that science is the human ability to understand and dominate nature, that it increases our material prosperity and security, and that it represents one of the pinnacles of human achievement. Its connotations are, therefore, of positive moral and functional values: it is good and useful. There is, of course a counter-myth with appropriate counter-connotations current amongst the ecology/conservationist subculture, but our dominant myth contains the sort of concepts outlined above.

These second-order meanings of science are produced by the dominant ideology of our culture, which sees history as progress, change as inevitable and for the better, which gives high priority to the improvement of material prosperity, and which is, finally, capitalist and competitive. But for a traditional agricultural community, such as the one shown in the film, these signs of science may well connote alienness, the not-to-be-trusted. They may well activate a myth of science as 'their magic; powerful but not ours', and they may not fit at all into an ideology that rates most highly tried and tested ways, the authority of the elders and ancestors, the continuation of a community and a way of life rather than change and improvement, and that sees history as cyclical, not as a progressive development.

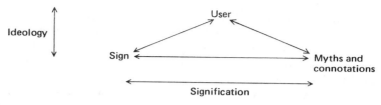

Figure 28

Ideology and signification

This programme is not special or particularly biased. It is, like all other acts of communication, taking part in the normal ideological process of signification. Central to this process are the connoted values and myths common to the members of a culture. The only way their commonality can be established and maintained is by their frequent use in communication. Every time a sign is used it reinforces the life of its second-order meanings both in the culture and in the user. So we have a triangular model of interrelationships as in figure 28. The interrelationships indicated by the double-ended arrows all depend upon frequent use for their existence and development. The user of the sign keeps it in currency by using it, and maintains the myths and connoted values of the culture only by responding to their use in communication. The relationship between the sign and its myths and connotations, on the one hand, and the user, on the other, is an ideological one.

Signs give myths and values concrete form and in so doing both endorse them and make them public. In using the signs we maintain and give life to the ideology, but we are also formed by that ideology, and by our response to ideological signs. When signs make myths and values public, they enable them to perform their function of cultural identification: that is, they enable members of a culture to identify their membership of that culture through their acceptance of common, shared myths and values. I know that I am a member of my western culture because, to give one of many identifications, I understand science with the same myths and endow it with the same connoted values as the majority of other inhabitants of the western world. I share an ideology with my fellows. In concrete terms, I connote plates 15a and b with positive values, with high status and believability. I do not read (as is easily possible) the foregrounding of the scientific apparatus in 15b as connoting that science is overpowering man. My ideology determines the meanings which I find in my interaction with those signs. The connotators and myths are, in Barthes's phrase, 'the rhetoric of my ideology'.

171

Ideology, then, in this third use, is not a static set of values and ways of seeing, but a practice. Ideology constitutes me as a particular member of my western science-based culture by the very fact that I am able to use and respond appropriately to signs, connotations, and myths. In participating in the signifying practice of my culture I am the means by which ideology maintains itself. The meanings I find in a sign derive from the ideology within which the sign and I exist: by finding these meanings I define myself in relation to the ideology and in relation to my society.

This discussion of the ideology of science might be read to imply that all partake of it equally, that science is socially neutral, and that the benefits of a science-based society are equally distributed. This, of course, is not so. Science and technology are intimately bound up with patriarchal capitalism. It is not just that science is used to increase the profits of big business and the middle classes who benefit most from them, but that science is one of the ways of exercising a more indefinable social power. Scientists are trained by universities, and those who succeed best in the university system tend to come from middle-class families: the highly-educated not only become the dominant class; they come from it, too. So science helps to maintain the current power structure.

Science is active in gender politics as well as class politics. Far more men than women are scientists in our society: this has nothing to do with innate or natural differences between men and women, but is part of the social, and therefore ideological, differences between masculinity and femininity. Science is ultimately a means of exerting power over the physical world; so, in a society where men exert power in the social world, it seems 'natural' that this power should be extended to the physical as well. The dominant sense of the women scientists that there are (unless they are in 'caring' or 'nurturing' sciences such as medicine) is that they are unfeminine, or, at least, unusual. This is ideology at its work of making the existing distribution of power in society appear 'normal' and 'natural'.

This view of ideology as an active political force in society rather than a set of ideas or a way of thinking is taken up more fully in the next section. For while ideology *is* a way of making sense, the sense that it makes always has a social and political dimension. Ideology, in this view, is a social practice.

Understanding ideology

The theory of ideology as a practice was developed by Louis Althusser

Speak Semiotics you damn fool!

(1971), a second-generation Marxist who had been influenced by the ideas of Saussure and Freud, and who thus brought theories of structure and of the unconscious to bear upon Marx's more economistic theories. For Marx, ideology was a relatively straightforward concept. It was the means by which the ideas of the ruling classes became accepted throughout society as natural and normal. All knowledge is class-based: it has inscribed within it its class origins and it works to prefer the interests of that class. Marx understood that the members of the subordinate class, that is the working class, were led to understand their social experience, their social relationships, and therefore themselves by means of a set of ideas that were not *theirs*, that came from a class whose economic, and therefore political and social, interests not only differed from theirs but were actively opposed to them.

According to Marx the ideology of the bourgeoisie kept the workers, or proletariat, in a state of *false consciousness*. People's consciousness of who they are, of how they relate to the rest of society, and therefore of the sense they make of their social experience is produced by society, not by nature or biology. Our consciousness is determined by the society we have been born into, not by our nature or individual psychology.

In the photograph of the clash between blacks and police in chapter 6 we can trace an example of this theory in practice. Members of the subordinated classes, whether black or white, who made sense of this photograph by the 'ideas of the ruling classes' (that is by white, middle-class myths) would have a 'false consciousness' not only of the photograph and the events it depicts but also of themselves and their social relations. These 'ruling-class ideas' propose that the meaning of the incident is to be found in the nature of young blacks – they are 'naturally' aggressive, disorderly, and unlawful – and that the police are the impartial agents of a law that is objective and equally fair to all classes in society. Their consciousness is thus 'bourgeois', and the photograph 'produces' its readers as bourgeois subjects who accept their relationship to the socio-economic system as fair and natural, and who therefore make 'common-sense' meanings of social experience such as this incident. This is a false consciousness because it denies the 'true' meaning that such conflict is caused by social relationships, not by the nature of blacks: their bitterness is caused by their position in a society that consistently disadvantages them and privileges middle-class whites. This consciousness cannot see the police as they 'really' are – the agents of a law designed to preserve the interests of those with property and power and thus to maintain the status quo against any force of social change.

The concept of ideology as false consciousness was so important in Marx's theory because it appeared to explain why it was that the majority in capitalist societies accepted a social system that disadvantaged them. Marx believed, however, that economic 'reality' was more influential, at least in the long run, than ideology, and that inevitably the workers would overthrow the bourgeoisie and produce a society where one class did not dominate and exploit the majority and so would not need to keep them in a state of false consciousness. In a fair and equal society there is no need for ideology because everyone will have a 'true' consciousness of themselves and their social relations. The bitterness of the black youths would be seen in this theory as a sign that their socio-economic 'reality' was stronger than the attempt of the dominant ideology to make them accept it.

As the twentieth century progressed, however, it became more and more clear that capitalism was not going to be overthrown by internal revolution, and that the socialist revolution in Russia was not going to spread to the rest of Europe and the western world. Yet capitalism still disadvantaged the majority of its members and exploited them for the benefit of a minority. To help account for this, Marxist thinkers such as Althusser (1971) developed a more sophisticated theory of ideology that freed it from such a close cause-and-effect relationship with the economic base of society, and redefined it as an ongoing and all-pervasive set of practices in which all classes participate, rather than a set of ideas imposed by one class upon the other. The fact that all classes participate in these practices does not mean that the practices themselves no longer serve the interests of the dominant, for they most certainly do: what it means is that ideology is much more effective than Marx gave it credit for because it works from within rather than without – it is deeply inscribed in the ways of thinking and ways of living of all classes.

A pair of high-heel shoes, to take an example, does not impose upon women from outside the ideas of the ruling gender (men); but wearing them is an ideological practice of patriarchy in which women participate, possibly even more than the ideology would require. Wearing them accentuates the parts of the female body that patriarchy has trained us into thinking of as attractive to men – the buttocks, thighs, and breasts. The woman thus participates in constructing herself as an attractive object for the male look, and therefore puts herself under the male power (of granting or withholding approval). Wearing them also limits her physical activity and strength – they hobble her and make her move precariously; so wearing them is practising the subordination of women in patriarchy. A woman in high heels is active in reproducing and recirculating the patriarchal meanings of gender that propose masculinity as stronger and more active, and femininity as weaker and more passive.

One of the most ubiquitous and insidious ideological practices is what Althusser calls 'interpellation' or 'hailing'. It is particularly relevant to this book because it is practised in every act of communication. All communication addresses someone, and in addressing them it places them in a social relationship. In recognizing ourself as the addressee and in responding to the communication, we participate in our own social, and therefore ideological, construction. If you hear in the street a shout 'Hey you!', you can either turn in the belief that you are being addressed or you can ignore it because you know that 'nobody, but *nobody*' speaks to you like that: you thus reject the relationship implicit in the call. All communication interpellates or hails us in some way: a pair of high-heel shoes, for example, hails the woman (or man) who 'answers' them by liking or wearing them as a patriarchal subject. The woman who recognizes 'herself' as their addressee by wearing them positions herself submissively within gender relations; the man who likes to see her wearing them is equally but differently positioned – he is hailed as one with power.

Similarly, if we allow ourselves to be spoken to or hailed by the advertisement in plate 9 (p. 99) we adopt the social position of a masculine middle-class subject. Accepting the idea of the feminine as the pure and the masculine as the snake-like corruptor, and taking as 'common sense' that the man is the seducer and the woman the seducee, is a patriarchal practice. Using a sophisticated, exotic drink as a sign of one's role in this practice gives it a particular bourgeois inflection. The advertisement invites us, whether we are men or women, to identify with the masculine way of making sense of the snake, the alcohol, and the seduction, and therefore of ourselves: we thus become the reader hailed by the advertisement. This is an important point to make, for it shows that interpellation can position us in an ideological category that may differ from our actual social one. So women can be positioned 'as men' to make masculine sense of themselves and their social relations, blacks can be positioned as whites, the working class as middle class, and so on. Communication is a social process and must therefore be ideological: interpellation is a key part of its ideological practice.

Althusser's theory of ideology as practice is a development of Marx's theory of it as false consciousness, but still emphasizes its role of maintaining the power of the minority over the majority by non-coercive means. Another European second-generation Marxist, Antonio Gramsci, introduced into this area another term – *hegemony*, which we might like to think of as ideology as struggle. Briefly, hegemony involves the constant winning and rewinning of the consent of the majority to the system that subordinates them. The two elements that Gramsci emphasizes more than Marx or Althusser are resistance and instability.

Hegemony is necessary, and has to work so hard, because the social experience of subordinated groups (whether by class, gender, race, age, or any other factor) constantly contradicts the picture that the dominant ideology paints for them of themselves and their social relations. In other words, the dominant ideology constantly meets resistances that it has to overcome in order to win people's consent to the social order that it is promoting. These resistances may be overcome, but they are never eliminated. So any hegemonic victory, any consent that it wins, is necessarily unstable; it can never be taken for granted, so it has to be constantly rewon and struggled over.

One of the key hegemonic strategies is the construction of 'common sense'. If the ideas of the ruling class can be accepted as *common* (i.e. not class-based) sense, then their ideological object is achieved and their ideological work is disguised. It is, for example, 'common sense' in our society that criminals are wicked or deficient individuals who need punishment or correction. Such common sense disguises the fact that lawbreakers are disproportionately men from disadvantaged or disempowered social groups – they are of the 'wrong' race, class, or age. Common sense thus rules out the possible sense that the causes of criminality are social rather than individual, that our society teaches men that their masculinity depends upon successful performance (which is typically measured by material rewards and social esteem), and then denies many of them the means of achieving this success. The 'law-abiding citizens', who 'happen', generally, to belong to those classes which have many avenues to socially successful performance, are thus relieved of the responsibility of thinking that criminality may be the product of the system that provides them with so many advantages, and that the solution to the problem may involve them in forgoing some of their privileges. The common sense that criminality is a function of the wicked individual rather than the unfair society is thus part of bourgeois ideology, and, in so far as it is accepted by the subordinate (and even by the criminals themselves, who may well believe that they deserve their punishment and that the criminal justice system is therefore fair to all), it is hegemony at work. Their consent to the common wisdom is a hegemonic victory, if only a momentary one.

Ideological theories stress that all communication and all meanings have a socio-political dimension, and that they cannot be understood outside their social context. This ideological work always favours the status quo, for the classes with power dominate the production and distribution not only of goods but also of ideas and meanings. The economic system is organized in their interest, and the ideological system derives from it and works to promote, naturalize, and disguise it. Whatever their differences, all ideological theories agree that ideology works to maintain class domination; their differences lie in the ways in which this domination is exercised, the degree of its effectiveness, and the extent of the resistances it meets.

To summarize it briefly, we may say that Marx's theory of ideology as false consciousness tied it closely to the economic base of society and posited that its falseness to the material conditions of the working class would inevitably result in the overthrow of the economic order that produced it. He saw it as the imposition of the ideas of the dominant minority upon the subordinate majority. This majority must eventually see through this false consciousness and change the social order that imposes it upon them.

Althusser's theory of ideology as practice, however, appeared to see no limits to ideology, neither in its reach into every aspect of our lives, nor historically. Its power lay in its ability to engage the subordinate in its practices and thus to lead them to construct social identities or subjectivities for themselves that were complicit with it, and against their own socio-political interests. The logical conclusion of his theory is that there is no way of escaping ideology, for although our material social experience may contradict it, the only means we have of making sense of that experience are always ideologically loaded; so the only sense we can make of our selves, our social relations, and our social experience is one that is a practice of the dominant ideology.

Gramsci's theory of hegemony, or ideology as struggle, however, lays far greater emphasis on resistance. While in broad agreement with

177

Althusser that the subordinate may consent to the dominant ideology and thus participate in its propagation, his theory also insists that their material social conditions contradict that dominant sense, and thus produce resistances to it. His account of the structures of domination is as subtle and convincing as Althusser's; but because he lays greater stress on the resistances that ideology has to overcome, but can never eliminate, his theory is finally the more satisfying, for it takes into account more of the contradictions that go to make up our social experience. Gramsci's theory makes social change appear possible, Marx's makes it inevitable, and Althusser's improbable.

Ideological analysis

Plate 16 is from the magazine *Seventeen*, which is aimed, in the words on its cover, at 'where the girl ends and the woman begins'. To assist its readers in crossing this boundary between girl and woman it circulates a set of meanings of femininity that are made to appear attractive and realistic to young women, yet finally serve the interests of those with power, that is middle-class men, a group whose interests are opposed to those of the readers addressed by this page.

Let us begin the analysis with the most obvious, for semiotics teaches us that what is most obvious and ordinary is where the greatest cultural significance lies: Althusser and Gramsci have both alerted us to the ideological work performed by 'common sense', a work performed by the phrase itself, for its sense is, of course, not 'common' but class-based, however well disguised its class origin in the ideas of the ruling class. The most obvious aspect of this page is its emphasis on appearance and domesticity and the linking of the two. What the page is saying is that women *are* what they look like, and what they look like is seen through the eyes of a man, ultimately a husband. Women are thus encouraged to see (make sense of) themselves through the eyes of another gender, the ruling gender. The central column of this page leads the eye down from a representation of the (ideal) family in a still from an early TV series *The Waltons*, through a cookbook of 'Mom-style' recipes to 'June Cleaver fever' – a young girl dressed in a traditional polka-dot fabric and a white frilly apron, but with a hint of sexual abandon in the 'loose' strands of hair and the thigh-revealing twirl of the hips. The words anchor the apron as the key sign in the photograph: 'Aprons aren't just for cooking any more. Aka [alias] pinafores, they're soft, flirty, and, well, very girlish.' The coy, hesitant commas reproduce the uncertainty and hesitancy of young women and hail the reader as a teenage girl. Pinafores

**NATURAL
AWARE
TRUTH
REAL**

N
(E)XT

Girls 'n' wear it
Welcome back,
Happy Face!
Stick him all
over a denim
jacket, or tie on
a smiley scarf.

Don't worry, be hippie
The '60s attitude is
back—in clothes, mu-
sic, food, and social
awareness. Tie-dyed
shirts remade for the
'80s in sheer fabrics
Powder boom The
"I never wear make-
up" look is fresh with
the new sheer powders.
Just like Mom's
Believe it or not, eat-
ing at home, à la
the Waltons, is
back in vogue.
Try the *Comfort
Food* cookbook
for Mom-style
recipes. Pass the
peas, John Boy.
The age of aquatics
The shore thing: pearls,
shells, and sea horses
sprinkled over jewelry.
Ecology rock
Rock 'n' rap groups get
into the clean-air act.
Watch for ads on TV
called "Pollution Solu-
tions," featuring D.J.
Jazzy Jeff & The
Fresh Prince.
**June Cleaver
fever**
Aprons aren't just
for cooking any-
more. Aka pin-
afores, they're
soft, flirty, and,
well, very girlish.
**Next year's
model**
We predict Christina
Khuly (far left) will be
on the covers of all the
top fashion magazines.

Seventeen—January 1982

COMFORT FOOD

Home cooking

"The rain forest of
South America is re-
sponsible for the air
we breathe. And it is
being destroyed. If
you're in school,
why not start a letter-
writing campaign to
stop this destruction
and to make this planet
a much better place."
Bob Weir, member of
The Grateful Dead
For info, write Creating
Our Future, 398 North Ferri-
daris, Mill Valley, CA 94941.

POLLUTION SOLUTION

Plate 16 *Seventeen*

and aprons are the same garment, but a pinafore is its childish version, and apron its adult: it thus straddles the categories of girl and woman. Its function is to keep the female looking clean. (Boys are allowed to get dirty, for dirt goes with masculine activity and with not caring about appearance so much, for masculinity is defined by what boys *do*, not by what they look like. Dirt is thus what males produce and females clean up). A pinafore keeps a girl clean from the dirt of play; an apron guards a woman from the dirt of work; but both preserve the clean appearance of the feminine, so girls' play slides easily into women's work (as it does on the cover of the cookbook). The girl thus 'naturally' becomes the woman whose work has produced the enormous amount of food necessary to feed the family in the top picture. This food will then be distributed by the man as though it were *his*, and woman's labour is thus made invisible: woman's work is what enables the man to preside over the family. The 'flirtiness' of the bottom picture is simply there to catch the man whom the woman will nurture and serve for the rest of her life.

In the left-hand column three young women define themselves by their appearance. Each presents herself for the camera, acknowledging it and her role, which is to be 'that which is photographed'; none of them is *doing* anything, but all are simply *being* their appearance. And this appearance is one of passivity, childishness, and submissiveness. Their facial features are reduced to eyes and mouths: the photograph at the bottom is lit so as to flatten out all other features, and the make-up and expression of all three models does the same. Emphasizing eyes and mouth is a way of 'infantilizing' the subject, just as 'cute' drawings of babies, puppies, kittens, calves, or baby bluebirds signify their helplessness by giving them huge eyes and cute mouths. Make-up and photographic conventions reproduce meanings of childishness upon the female face. The bodily postures do the same, for they all tilt or lower the body into what Goffman (1979), in his detailed analysis of gender portrayal in advertisements, characterizes as a submissive body cant. These postures address a powerful upright male from a position of submission.

The centre one is particularly infantilized. The 'Happy Face' badge is a childish drawing which, like the photographs, reduces the face to eyes and mouth, and the model is the youngest looking or most tomboyish of the three. The other two have signs of more mature sexuality grafted on to the basic childishness, so the 'play' fashion of the badges on the centre model slides into the more 'adult' fashion of the tie-dyed shirt in sheer fabric of the top one, and her childishly dishevelled hair becomes the sophisticatedly unkempt look of the bottom model. This reproduces the merging in the centre column of girl's play into women's work; so, the implication is, fashion (or appearance) *is* women's work – they need to nurture the vision of the male by looking stylish for him just as much as to nurture his body by cooking for him.

The right-hand column is more complex and contradictory. One of its ideological functions is to transfer the meanings of the title words NATURAL AWARE TRUTH REAL to the meanings of femininity proposed by the other columns. The concern with ecology and pollution is being 'aware' of the 'real truth' of 'nature' (or of the 'true nature of reality' or the 'natural real truth' – it is the association of the concepts that matters, not their grammatical order). The unstated and repressed worry of the page is that some readers may consider that make-up and fashion are unnatural, and may even be thought to pollute the true, real female body. The potential concern that a reader might feel about this is *displaced* on to a concern for the environment. ('Displacement' is a term that ideological theories have borrowed from Freudian dream theory: when a topic or anxiety is repressed, either psychologically or ideologically, the concern for it can only be expressed by being *displaced* on to a legitimate, socially acceptable topic.) Concern for the environment is admirable, and its social acceptability is what makes it such an effective displacement. This displaced relationship between make-up and pollution underlies the 'I never wear make-up look' of the new sheer powders, for they are invisible and thus do not pollute the nature of the face – they are ecologically sound!

Another term used in ideological analysis is *incorporation*. This refers to the process by which the dominant classes take elements of resistance from the subordinate and use them to maintain the status quo, rather than to challenge it. They incorporate resistances into the dominant ideology and thus deprive them of their oppositionality. 'Don't worry, be hippie. The '60s attitude is back – in clothes, music, food, and social awareness' is an example of incorporation. The social movements of the 1960s, from the freedom rides against racism in the US South to the worldwide protests against the Vietnam War and the student anti-government demonstrations that swept Europe and the US, have all been reduced to fashion, musical style, and the safe, respectable social awareness of ecology. There is no sense here that the social awareness of the sixties, for instance, could result in the National Guard firing on an unarmed demonstration at Kent State University and killing four students. The political oppositionality of that decade has been defused and incorporated into the dominant ideology.

Rock and roll, too, often has oppositional meanings for its fans, but this, too, is defused as it is incorporated into the socially acceptable concerns of ecology and anti-pollution movements. By linking these social movements to a concern for nature, incorporation disguises or masks the political fact that it is capitalism that causes the pollution – something that the hippies in the sixties were well aware of, but which is significantly absent from the *Seventeen* page (*masking* and *significant absences* are two other common terms in ideological analysis). The Grateful Dead, too, have been incorporated. To their original fans, and to most of their present ones, they were an oppositional band, promoting alternative life-styles, oppositional values, and anti-capitalist meanings. For this page, however, unlike the culture of the sixties and the 'original' Grateful Dead that it refers to and incorporates, there is nothing wrong with capitalism: indeed, capitalism, far from being the problem, is the implied solution, for it is capitalism that produces the commodities a girl needs in order to turn her appearance (i.e. 'herself') from that of a girl to that of a woman, and which she will need in order to run a home for her husband and children, and thus to enable her to become the woman she 'really is'. Masking ecology under a concern for nature instead of mobilizing it as a protest against capitalism is another ideological practice of this page.

Yet another is commodification. Capitalism is the system that, above all others, produces commodities, so making commodities seem natural is at the heart of much ideological practice. We learn to understand our desires in terms of the commodities produced to meet them; we learn to think of our problems in terms of the commodities by which to solve them. So the problems of maturing from a girl to a woman are framed and solved in terms of commodities – apron, cookbooks, happy badges, hair styles, clothes, make-up. The problems of relating our artificial society to nature and thus making it appear natural are commodified – we sprinkle natural pearls, shells, or sea-horses on jewellery, and advertising (*the* commodity art form) serves ecology with television ads called 'Pollution Solutions'. The photograph from *The Waltons* defines the family by its commodities – the large, expensive table which expresses family unity by allowing them all to sit at once; the large, comfortable house; their respectable clothes; the flowers, plates, and silverware on the table – the whole sense of middle-class prosperity becomes essential to the meaning of family in capitalism. They are a family which *consumes*; they are a commodified family. (Taking the photograph out of its original context masks the fact that the series was set in the Depression and that one of its main themes was coping with poverty. The photograph works to deny politically oppositional readings of *The Waltons* and to incorporate the family into unproblematic commodity capitalism.)

The rest of the magazine is, of course, full of advertisements, fashion and make-up features, advice columns, and fiction that all promote commodities, and therefore the economic interests of those who produce and distribute them. Women's bodies and their lives are constructed as a set of problems for which there are commodities to provide solutions: this page is a microcosm of the magazine. And the magazine is, of course, the most important commodity of all. Its strongly flagged concern for the interests of its young readers is actually a way of constructing those interests as ones that can be met by the appropriate commodities – itself included. So its young readers are led to construct its interests as theirs in much the same way that Marx argues that ideology made the workers adopt the consciousness of the bourgeoisie, or that Morley found that women adopted masculine values to disparage their own taste in television.

What Barthes calls the *myths* of femininity and family work, as do all myths, to turn history and society into nature. Thus the myths allow for no differences between the Waltons and a present-day family, no differences between today's reader and her parents' generation in the sixties, no differences between the daughter and mother on the cookbook, nor between the girls and women throughout this page. Nor, finally, do they allow for any difference of interests between the producers and readers of this page. Such differences are historically and socially produced, and they are thus masked by the way that myth naturalizes meanings. So the myth says that girls 'naturally' become women who 'naturally' become housewives, and thus it makes significantly absent any question of what sort of women they become and whose interests are served by this. Naturalizing the existing order makes it appear universal and therefore unchangeable (like nature); the problem is not how to change the social system, but how to insert oneself into it (with the aid of the right commodities) and thus how to maintain it.

Women's pleasures (of being flirty when young and maternal when older) and the commodities by which to achieve them are produced by the system of patriarchal capitalism that ensures the subordination of women; and in so far as women accept these commodified pleasures and experience them as real, they are actively promoting an ideology that is against their interests: they are participating in hegemony. By recognizing herself as the addressee 'hailed' by this page, the reader is practising patriarchal ideology; and by accepting the common sense of the representations of herself and her future, she is helping to win the consent of herself and others like her to a system that only middle-class men can benefit from in the long run.

Resistances

This page from *Seventeen* is a good example of hegemony at work, but hegemony has to work so hard because so much of the day-to-day

183

experience of young women contradicts it. Hegemony is the means by which their consent to the system that disadvantages them is won, but its victories are never complete or stable: because of the contradictory experiences of everyday life the struggle is never over, and any ground won by the dominant ideology has to be constantly defended and actively held on to.

The ideological theories of Marx and Althusser are useful in revealing how ubiquitous and insidious the workings of the dominant ideology are, but this emphasis leads them to ignore or underestimate the extent of its struggle and the resistance it meets. Both theories tend to assume that ideological power is well-nigh irresistible. Ideological analysis, therefore, tends to focus on the coherence of texts, the way that all their elements come together to tell the same story, that of white, patriarchal capitalism. The theory of hegemony, however, extends this focus on the forces of domination by encouraging us to look for moments of weakness in texts, for contradictions in their ideological smoothness and coherence. While recognizing that these forces will always attempt to incorporate resistance, it doubts the final effectiveness of this strategy and argues that some traces of that resistance will necessarily remain. These contradictions and traces of resisting meanings may be identified by a hegemonic analysis of texts, but whether or not they are actually taken up and acted upon can be established only by ethnographic study.

The 'no make-up look' is a strategy to incorporate the resistance of many young women to the ideological practice of painting their faces. Many feel that making-up is selling out to the system and that in practising it they are selling themselves short by accepting a social identity or sense of self that is not theirs. Traces of this point of view, with its resistance to both capitalism and patriarchy, remain on the *Seventeen* page and are available to promote oppositional readings of it.

Similarly, the model in the top left-hand picture is wearing torn jeans. Torn jeans can be a sign of resistance to the dominant ideology − they are kept longer than normal so that the purchase of a new pair is delayed, a small but significant resistance to commodification. They also oppose the idea that 'respectable' girls (i.e. those marriageable by equally respectable men) should be clean, neat, and well dressed. They offer at least a hint of meanings that oppose the ones preferred so assiduously by the rest of this page.

Elsewhere (Fiske 1989a) I report on an ethnographic study of the ideological practices involved in wearing jeans. It emerged that wearing them works to circulate three main sets or clusters of meanings. The first is their association with hard work and hard leisure, with activity and with the dignity of labour, particularly of working for oneself. The second is a set of associations clustered around the American West – freedom, naturalness, ruggedness, informality, self-sufficiency, tradition. And finally there are meanings of Americanness and social consensus. Jeans are the US's unique contribution to the international fashion scene. They are consensual in that they can be worn by both genders, by all classes, races, and ages – they transcend all social categories and carry the myth that in America all are free, equal individuals. So, for those whose gender and age (not to mention race or class) tell them that they are not as free and equal as others and lead them to wish to contradict some of the dominant meanings of jeans, tearing them can be a sign of resistance to the dominant ideology. Of course, the industry reacts to this and attempts to incorporate such resistance by producing designer-torn (or faded) jeans, but such 'designer-wear' and 'genuine' wear are still different, and the differences are recognized by the wearers of each: some of the resistance always remains finally unincorporable.

The girl on the middle left of the magazine page wears a 'unisex', tomboyish set of jeans – which is appropriate in that she is the youngest of the women shown and is thus closest to pre-puberty, when gender difference is least marked. But she is still clearly a post-pubertal young woman, and so her signs of refusing gender differences may also contain hints of resistance to the ideologically restricted meanings of femininity that the rest of the page is promoting.

If this page is to be popular, if it is to hail its intended readers accurately, it must contain some signs of their oppositional social position as well as the voice of the dominant ideology. Without such contradictions many of its targeted readers might not recognize themselves as its addressees; they would thus refuse its interpellation and it would fail to communicate with them. The page must contradict itself in the same way that the social experience of the subordinate contradicts the meanings that the dominant ideology proposes for them. Hegemony theory argues that the ideological work of this page to win the consent of young women to patriarchal capitalism is not just an ideological practice but an ideological struggle, and that signs of the resistances it has to overcome can never be wiped out, that some always remain to fuel more resistance in the future. The consent of the subordinate to the dominant system is never finally won; always elements of grudgingness or resistance remain, and the degree of consent will vary considerably among the readers of this page. Hegemony theory allows for less traditional, more rebellious, meanings of young-womanhood to challenge, and possibly even modify, the dominant ones. It is thus both more optimistic and

INTRODUCTION TO COMMUNICATION STUDIES

more progressive than those theories that focus exclusively on the
dominant ideology.

Suggestions for further work

1. Make a semiotic analysis of the advertisement in plate 17. Pay
    particular attention to the second order of signification: show how
    this order can be meaningful only within a particular ideology. You
    should discuss the ideology of the family, of masculinity, femininity,
    and gender roles, of nature *v.* the city, of leisure *v.* work, of

Plate 17   *'Go Native'*

consumption *v*. production, and of class dominance.

This should produce a preferred reading according to the dominant code. Now produce a negotiated reading; one appropriate to, say, a dedicated hill-walker who loves nature in general and the Yorkshire Dales in particular, but would never use nature in the antiseptic, suburban manner of the family shown. Devise other negotiated readings and readers. Remember that a negotiated reading accepts and works within the dominant ideology, but negotiates a different stance towards, or a more privileged place for, certain topics, beliefs, or groups of people.

Outline an ideology that would produce a radically opposed reading for this advertisement, or one that would render it meaningless (or almost).

Discuss the role of semiotic analysis in discovering, or making visible, ideological practice. Does an awareness of the preference of certain readings over others and of the ideological system within which this preference works provide us with a defence against constant indoctrination by the dominant ideology? Does it make such an indoctrination impossible (in that it has to work below the threshold of awareness to be effective)? Or does it simply offer us the choice of accepting or rejecting the preferred reading? Does semiotic analysis necessarily have a political or moral dimension?

Further reading: Dyer (1982), chapter 6; Hartley (1982), chapters 3 and 9; Williamson (1978), pp. 40–5, 122–37; Morley (1980), pp. 16–21, 134; Barthes (1977), pp. 32–51.

2. Take plates 1a and b, 11a and b, and 18. The photographs in plates 1a and 11a were published in the press (after considerable editorial treatment); the one in plate 18 was not. Why not? Using these five plates as your data discuss the topic 'Ideology and the representation of the police in the media'. You should use Barthes's theory of the second order of signification as the 'rhetoric of ideology', and you should compare and contrast the 'professional ideology' of the newsmen and news values with the 'dominant ideology' of the culture as a whole. Design a page layout and caption that would allow the use of plate 18 in a mass-circulation British paper. Give reasons for your editorial decisions and show how they take account of your understanding of ideology. Show also that you understand the interaction of words with visual image.

Plate 18   *Police and girl*

(Photograph by Eve Arnold from the British Journal of Photography Annual 1973)

CONCLUSION

And so we draw towards the end. And it is therefore time to refer back to the Introduction, to clarify how we started on our approach to the study of communication. The process school, with its common-sense model of communication, has many attractions. It appears more functional; it can encourage us to improve our skills of communication which will then enable us to impose ourselves on the world around us more effectively. It sees communication as a determinant, and improving communication as a way of increasing social control. Hence its attractive and interesting studies of the audience, of the effects of communication. It is, to put it succinctly, the advertising executive's view.

But semiotics, deriving largely from Saussure and Peirce, is concerned not with the transmission of messages but with the generation and exchange of meanings. The emphasis here is not on stages in the process, but on the text and its interaction with its producing/receiving culture: the focus is on the role of communication in establishing and maintaining values and on how those values enable communication to have meaning. Saussure's and Peirce's interest in the nature of the sign itself, rather than in how it is transmitted, signals this change of focus. This school has no concept of a breakdown in communication and is not much concerned with efficiency and accuracy. Communication must occur: a case in which my meaning differs from your meaning is not seen as a communication failure, but as indicative of social or cultural differences between us. And divergence of meanings is not necessarily, of itself, a bad thing: it may, indeed, be a source of cultural richness and of subcultural maintenance. If we wish to minimize the divergence of meanings we should not, according to this school, seek to achieve this by improving the efficiency of the communication process, but by minimizing the social differences. In other words, the determinants of communication lie in society and the world around us, not in the process itself.

This means, of course, that cultural and social differences must inevitably produce what the process school would see as breakdowns in communication. In industrial organizations, to take a fraught and topical example, disputes are frequently blamed on a breakdown in communication. This is a process-school explanation. A semiotician would say that there is no such thing as a breakdown of communication: when the workforce find a meaning that is different from that of management in the words or actions of managers, this is a manifestation of socio-cultural differences: it is, itself, a message about social relations within the firm and within society, and will not therefore be put right by improvements in the efficiency of the communication process.

Another currently topical example is that of televised violence. The process-school proponents see a direct linear link between violence in the television message and its effect of causing violence in the receiver. Semioticians would argue that if the reader is moved to violence, then we must look for the causes of violence in his or her socio-cultural experience as well as in the television message, and that no amount of change of this television message will, by itself, reduce violence in society.

It is not my intention to suggest that there is a right and a wrong way to study communication. But there are ways that are more or less fruitful. In my opinion the semiotic school addresses itself to the more important questions in communication, and is the more useful in helping us to understand the myriad examples that we meet with in our daily lives. But I certainly do not think that it can provide all the answers. The more empirical work of the process school is often needed to fill dangerous gaps left by semiotics. It is a pity that proponents of each school have tended to ignore or denigrate the work of the other: I am pleased that some recent work (such as that by Gerbner or Morley) is showing signs that the two can be brought closer together. I hope that this book will also contribute to this end.

REFERENCES

Abercrombie, M. (1960) *The Anatomy of Judgement*, London: Hutchinson.

Althusser, L. (1971) 'Ideology and ideological state apparatuses' in *Lenin and Philosophy and other Essays*, New York and London: Monthly Review Press, 127–86.

Argyle, M. (1972) 'Non-verbal communication in human social interaction' in Hinde, R. (ed.) (1972).

Baggaley, J. and Duck, S. (1976) *The Dynamics of Television*, Farnborough, Hants: Saxon House.

Barr, C. (1975) 'Comparing styles: England *v.* West Germany' in Buscombe, E. (ed.) (1975).

Barthes, R. (1968) *Elements of Semiology*, London: Cape.

—— (1973) *Mythologies*, London: Paladin.

—— (1977) *Image–Music–Text*, London: Fontana.

—— (1961) 'The photographic message' in Barthes (1977).

—— (1964) 'The rhetoric of the image' in Barthes (1977).

—— (1970) 'The third meaning' in Barthes (1977).

Benjamin, W. (1970) 'The work of art in the age of mechanical reproduction' in Curran, J., Gurevitch, M., and Woollacott, J. (eds.) (1977).

Bernstein, B. (1973) *Class, Codes, and Control* (vol. 1), London: Paladin.

—— (1964) 'Elaborated and restricted codes: their social origins and some consequences' in Smith, A. G. (ed.) (1966).

Blumler, J. and Katz, E. (eds.) (1974) *The Uses of Mass Communications*, Beverley Hills, California: Sage.

Brockreide, E. (1968) 'Dimensions of the concept of rhetoric' in Sereno, K. and Mortenson, C. D. (eds.) (1970) *Foundations of Communication*

Theory, New York: Harper & Row.

Buscombe, E. (ed.) (1975) *Football on Television*, London: British Film Institute.

Cherry, C. (1957) (2nd edn. 1966) *On Human Communication*, Cambridge, Mass.: MIT Press.

Cohen, S. and Young, J. (eds.) (1973) *The Manufacture of News*, London: Constable.

Corner, J. and Hawthorn, J. (eds.) (1980) *Communication Studies*, London: Arnold.

Culler, J. (1976) *Saussure*, London: Fontana.

Curran, J., Gurevitch, M., and Woollacott, J. (eds.) (1977) *Mass Communication and Society*, London: Arnold.

Dominick, J. and Rauch, G. (1972) 'The image of women in network TV commercials', *J. of Broadcasting*, 16, pp. 259–65.

Dyer, G. (1982) *Advertising as Communication*, London: Methuen.

Eco, U. (1965) 'Towards a semiotic inquiry into the TV message' (trans.), in *Working Papers in Cultural Studies*, University of Birmingham, No. 3 (1972), pp. 103–21; also in Corner, J. and Hawthorn, J. (eds.) (1980).

Evans, H. (1978) *Pictures on a Page*, London: Heinemann.

Fiske, J. (1987) *Television Culture*, London and New York: Methuen.

—— (1989a) *Understanding Popular Culture*, Boston: Unwin Hyman.

—— (1989b) *Reading the Popular*, Boston: Unwin Hyman.

—— (1979) 'Roland Barthes and the hidden curriculum', *J. Educational Television*, V:3, pp. 84–6.

Fiske, J. and Hartley, J. (1978) *Reading Television*, London: Methuen.

Fiske, J., Hodge, R., and Turner, G. (1987) *Myths of Oz: Readings in Australian Popular Culture*, Sydney: Allen and Unwin; Boston: Unwin Hyman.

de Fleur, M. (1964) 'Occupational roles as portrayed on television', *Public Opinion Quarterly*, 28, pp. 57–74.

Galtung, J. and Ruge, M. (1973) 'Structuring and selecting news' in Cohen, S. and Young, J. (eds.) (1973).

Gerbner, G. (1956). 'Toward a general model of communication', *Audio Visual Communication Review*, IV:3, pp. 171–99.

—— (1970) 'Cultural indicators: the case of violence in television drama', *Annals of the American Association of Political and Social Science*, 338, pp. 69–81.

—— (1973a) 'Cultural indicators: the third voice' in Gerbner, G., Gross, L., and Melody, T. (eds.) (1973).

—— (1973b) 'Teacher image in mass culture: symbolic functions of the "hidden curriculum" ' in Gerbner, G., Gross, L., and Melody, T. (eds.) (1973).

Gerbner, G. and Gross, L. (1976) 'Living with television: the violence profile', *J. of Communication*, 26:2, pp. 173–99.

Gerber, G., Gross, L., and Melody, T. (eds.) (1973) *Communication Technology and Social Policy*, New York: Wiley-Interscience.

Glasgow Media Group (1976) *Bad News*, London: Routledge & Kegan Paul.

—— (1980) *More Bad News*, London: Routledge & Kegan Paul.

Goffman, E. (1979) *Gender Advertisements*, London: Macmillan.

Guiraud, P. (1975) *Semiology*, London: Routledge & Kegan Paul.

Gusfield, J. and Schwartz, M. (1963) 'The meanings of occupational prestige', *American Sociological Review*, p. 270.

Hall, S. (1973a) 'Encoding and decoding in the television message' in Hall, S., Hobson, D., Lowe, A., and Willis, P. (eds.) (1980).

—— (1973b) 'The determinations of news photographs' in Cohen, S. and Young, J. (eds.) (1973).

Hall, S., Connell, I., and Curti, L. (1976). 'The "unity" of current affairs television' in *Working Papers in Cultural Studies*, University of Birmingham, No. 9, pp. 51–94.

Hall, S., Hobson, D., Lowe, A., and Willis, P. (eds.) (1980) *Culture, Media, Language*, London: Hutchinson.

Hartley, J. (1982) *Understanding News*, London: Methuen.

Hawkes, T. (1977) *Structuralism and Semiotics*, London: Methuen.

Head, S. (1954) 'Content analysis of television drama programs', *Quarterly of Film, Radio and Television*, 9:2, pp. 175–94.

Hinde, R. (ed.) (1972) *Non-Verbal Communication*, Cambridge: Cambridge University Press.

Hobson, D. (1982) *Crossroads: The Drama of a Soap Opera*, London: Methuen.

Hodge, R. and Tripp, D. (1986) *Children and Television*, Cambridge: Polity Press.

Jakobson, R. (1960) 'Closing statement: linguistics and poetics' in Sebeok, T. (ed.) (1960) *Style and Language*, Cambridge, Mass.: MIT Press; also in de George, R. and de George, F. (eds.) (1972) *The Structuralists from Marx to Lévi-Strauss*, New York: Doubleday, Anchor Books.

Jakobson, R. and Halle, M. (1956) *The Fundamentals of Language*, The Hague: Mouton.

Katz, E., Gurevitch, M., and Hass, E. (1973) 'On the uses of the mass media for important things', *American Sociological Review*, 38, pp. 164–81.

Kottak, P. (1982) *Researching American Culture*, Ann Arbor: University of Michigan Press.

Lakoff, G. and Johnson, M. (1980) *Metaphors We Live By*, Chicago: University of Chicago Press.

Lasswell, H. (1948) 'The structure and function of communication in society' in Bryson, L. (ed.) (1948) *The Communication of Ideas*, New York: Institute for Religious and Social Studies; also in Schramm, W. (ed.) (1960) *Mass Communications*, Illinois: University of Illinois Press.

Leach, E. (1974) *Lévi-Strauss*, London: Fontana.

—— (1976) *Culture and Communication*, London: Cambridge University Press.

—— (1964) 'Anthropological aspects of language: animal categories and verbal abuse' in E. Lennenberg (ed.) (1964) *New Directions in the Study of Language*, Cambridge, Mass.: MIT Press, pp. 23–63.

Leech, G. N. (1969) *A Linguistic Guide to English Poetry*, London: Longman.

Lévi-Strauss, C. (1969) *The Raw and the Cooked*, London: Cape.

McKeown, N. (1982) *Case Studies and Projects in Communication*, London: Methuen.

McLuhan, M. (1964) *Understanding Media*, London: Routledge & Kegan Paul.

—— (1967) *The Mechanical Bride*, London: Routledge & Kegan Paul.

McQuail, D. (ed.) (1972) *Sociology of Mass Communications*, Harmondsworth: Penguin.

—— (1975) *Communication*, London: Longman.

McQuail, D., Blumler, J., and Brown, R. (1972) 'The television audience: a revised perspective' in McQuail, D. (ed.) (1972).

Monaco, J. (1977) *How to Read a Film*, New York: Oxford University Press.

Morley, D. (1980) *The Nationwide Audience*, London: British Film Institute.

—— (1986) *Family Television*, London: Comedia/Methuen.

Newcomb, T. (1953) 'An approach to the study of communication acts', *Psychological Review*, 60, pp. 393–40; also in Smith, A. G. (ed.) (1966).

Ogden, C. and Richards, I. (1923; 2nd edn. 1949) *The Meaning of Meaning*, London: Routledge & Kegan Paul.

Osgood, C. (1967) *The Measurement of Meaning*, Illinois: University of Illinois Press.

Paisley, W. (1967) 'Studying style as a deviation from encoding norms' in Gerbner, G. *et al.* (eds.) (1969) *The Analysis of Communication*

Content, New York: Wiley.

Parkin, F. (1972) *Class Inequality and Political Order*, London: Paladin.

Peirce, C. S. (1931–58) *Collected Papers*, Cambridge, Mass.: Harvard University Press.

Radway, J. (1984) *Reading the Romance: Feminism and the Representation of Women in Popular Culture*, Chapel Hill: University of North Carolina Press.

de Saussure, F. (1974) (1st edn. 1915) *Course in General Linguistics*, London: Fontana.

Sebeok, T. (ed.) (1977) *A Perfusion of Signs*, Bloomington: Indiana University Press.

—— (ed.) (1978) *Sight, Sound and Sense*, Bloomington: Indiana University Press.

Seggar, J. and Wheeler, P. (1973) 'The world of work on television: ethnic and sex representation in TV drama', *J. of Broadcasting*, 17, pp. 201–14.

Shannon, C. and Weaver, W. (1949) *The Mathematical Theory of Communication*, Illinois: University of Illinois Press.

Smith, A. G. (ed.) (1966) *Communication and Culture*, New York: Holt, Rinehart & Winston.

Smythe, D. (1953) 'Three years of New York television', *National Association of Educational Broadcasters Monitoring Study*, No. 6, Urbana, Illinois.

Walker, M. (1978) *Daily Sketches: A Cartoon History of British Twentieth Century Politics*, London: Paladin.

Weaver, W. (1949a) 'Recent contributions to the mathematical theory of communication', Appendix to Shannon, C. and Weaver, W. (1949).

—— (1949b) 'The mathematics of communication', *Scientific American*, 181, pp. 11–15; also in Smith, A. G. (ed.) (1966).

Welch, R., Huston-Stein, A., Wright, J., and Plehal, R. (1979) 'Subtle sex role cues in children's commercials', *J. of Communications*, 29:3, pp. 202–9.

Westley, B. and MacLean, M. (1957) 'A conceptual model for communication research', *Journalism Quarterly*, 34, pp. 31–8.

Williams, R. (1977) *Marxism and Literature*, Oxford: Oxford University Press.

Williamson, J. (1978) *Decoding Advertisements*, London: Marion Boyars.

Woollacott, J. (1977) *Messages and Meanings*, Milton Keynes: The Open University Press (DE 353, Unit 6).

Wright, C. R. (1959) (2nd edn. 1975) *Mass Communications: A Sociological Approach*, New York: Random House.

Zeman, J. (1977) 'Peirce's theory of signs' in Sebeok, T. (ed.) (1977).

BIBLIOGRAPHY

Further reading

In addition to the other titles in this series, the following books are recommended for those who wish to read further into the issues raised in this volume.

Barthes, R. (1973) *Mythologies*, London: Paladin. An original, lively, sometimes difficult collection of essays on contemporary, very varied 'texts'. Read the first half of 'Myth today' at least – the second half is heavy going but worth the effort for serious students.

Barthes, R. (1977) *Image–Music–Text*, London: Fontana. Another collection of essays – 'The photographic message' and 'The rhetoric of the image' are not to be missed.

Cherry, C. (1957) (2nd edn. 1966) *On Human Communication*, Cambridge, Mass.: MIT Press. Early, comprehensive, though the mathematical angle has not proved as fruitful as was hoped – needs selective reading.

Cohen, S. and Young, J. (eds.) (1973) *The Manufacture of News*, London: Constable. A good selection of essays – specific, applied, theoretical, relevant, and sometimes funny: what more could you ask?

Corner, J. and Hawthorn, J. (eds.) (1980) *Communication Studies*, London: Arnold. A reader that makes a real attempt to cover the field; sections on: communication, definitions and approaches; perception, behaviour, interaction; language, thought, culture; meaning and interpretation; mass communication. Most of the major authorities are represented – a good support for this book.

Culler, J. (1976) *Saussure*, London: Fontana. A well-written account of the theories and significance of the great linguist.

Fiske, J. and Hartley, J. (1978) *Reading Television*, London: Methuen. Useful for its outline of semiotic theory and content analysis with examples. Applied, obviously, to television, but more widely applicable.

Guiraud, P. (1975) *Semiology*, London: Routledge & Kegan Paul. A short, useful little book that explains the main terms but is short on applied analysis. Rare in that it is an example of non-left-wing semiotics!

Hall, S., Hobson, D., Lowe, A., and Willis, P. (eds.) *Culture, Media, Language*, London: Hutchinson. A collection of some of the main work of the Birmingham Centre for Contemporary Cultural Studies. Some advanced work here, but important reading for the serious student. See especially the section on media studies.

Hawkes, T. (1977) *Structuralism and Semiotics*, London: Methuen. Literary in emphasis and examples, but gives a good account of the development and theory of semiotics.

McQuail, D. (1975) *Communication*, London: Longman. Comprehensive, sociological, not always easy reading but worth the effort for the theoretical framework it gives to the whole field.

Morley, D. (1980) *The Nationwide Audience*, London: British Film Institute. A highly recommended work, admirable in its combination of semiotic/cultural theory with empirical study.

Smith, A. G. (1966) *Communication and Culture*, New York: Holt, Rinehart & Winston. A large collection of essays – particularly useful for the number of models included. Essays by Weaver, Cherry, Newcomb, Westley and MacLean, Bernstein, Goffman, to name but a few. Not in paperback.

Webster, F. (1980) *The New Photography*, London: John Calder. This book is not specifically referred to in suggestions for further work, but it covers the reading of news photographs and advertisements. It is readable and thorough and can be recommended.

Books recommended for additional reading

Readers

Hinde, R. (ed.) (1972) *Non-Verbal Communication*, Cambridge: Cambridge University Press. Excellent collection of essays, mainly on communication, codes, and cultural background. See especially those by MacKay, Lyons, Argyle, Leach, Miller, and Gombrich.

Sereno, K. and Mortenson, C. D. (eds.) (1970) *Foundations of Communica-*

tion Theory, New York: Harper & Row. Another impressive collection of essays which illustrates the variety of approaches to the study of communication theory. Some are advanced, but most are easily readable. Sections include: perspectives, systems, decoding–encoding, interaction, and social context.

Curran, J., Gurevitch, M., and Woollacott, J. (eds.) (1977) *Mass Communication and Society*, London: Arnold. Excellent reader covering all the burning issues of media studies. The list of contributors reads like a *Who's Who* of media studies. Some very advanced reading, little at introductory level, but a goldmine for those prepared to dig.

McQuail, D. (ed.) (1972) *Sociology of Mass Communications*, Harmondsworth: Penguin. Good reader, more at the introductory level than Curran *et al.* (1977). A wide range of topics by a prestigious series of authors.

Buscombe, E. (ed.) (1975) *Football on Television*, London: British Film Institute. Cheap, readable little book – excellent for the way it exemplifies various methods of analysis. Should spark off numerous ideas for group and individual work. Recommended.

(*Note*: all the BFI Television Monographs are well worth reading and are excellent value for money.)

Textbooks

Lin, N. (1973) *The Study of Human Communication*, New York: Bobbs Merrill. Good textbook, especially strong on the linguistic, psychological, and social-psychological approaches. Scientific in style.

Mortenson, G. (1972) *Communication: The Study of Human Interaction*, New York: McGraw-Hill. Another good textbook in the 'transmission' school. Well illustrated, readable, more comprehensive than Lin (1973). Good introduction.

Semiotics

Monaco, J. (1977) *How to Read a Film*, New York: Oxford University Press. A thorough, well-illustrated review of semiotic theory and concepts, supported by ideas drawn from perception theory and applied to film. Good analysis of specifically filmic codes. Good alternative to Fiske, J. and Hartley, J. (1978).

Woollacott, J. (1977) *Messages and Meanings*, Milton Keynes: The Open

University Press (DE 353, Unit 6). A succinct account of the main theory and methods of semiotics; readable applied Marxism – can't be bad!

Mass media

Golding, P. (1974) *The Mass Media*, London: Longman. British version of Wright (1959) but shorter, more up-to-date, though lacking in any content study; but good.

Williams, R. (1962) (3rd edn. 1976) *Communications*, Harmondsworth: Penguin. Recommended brief book. Good history and very good chapter on content of the press that is crying out for comparisons with today's press.

Williams, R. (1974) *Television: Technology and Cultural Form*, London: Fontana. Good social/technological history followed by excellent chapters on the form and content of television; some American examples.

Wright, C. (1959) (2nd edn. 1975) *Mass Communication: A Sociological Approach*, New York: Random House. Good, readable introductory text, covering the functions, institutions, contents, and effects of the media, together with chapters on the communicators and the audience. Feels somewhat dated and locked into its sociological problem-free approach, but still a good point from which to start studies of the media.

Non-verbal communication

Argyle, M. (1972) (3rd edn. 1978) *The Psychology of Interpersonal Behaviour*, Harmondsworth: Penguin.

—— (1975) *Bodily Communication*, London: Methuen. Two key works by the leading British authority on the social psychological approach to the study of non-verbal communication. Both are readable, though the 1972 one is probably the easier way in. That of 1975 is broader and takes more account of the social/cultural context.

Hall, E. (1973) *The Silent Language*, New York: Anchor Books. A useful balance to Argyle: as an anthropologist Hall gives greater emphasis to the part played by culture in non-verbal communication.

INDEX

200